Blessed Are You the Poor!

Father Joseph Wresinski

Blessed Are You the Poor!

Translated by Alwine de Vos van Steenwijk
and Diana Skelton-Faujour
with acknowledgements to
Mr Rene Ochs and Ms Marie Ellen Mageveney for
their painstaking collaboration.

FOURTH WORLD
PUBLICATIONS

Original title: Heureux vous les pauvres
© Editions Cana, 75007 Paris, France.

This edition © Fourth World Publications 1992,
15, Rue Maitre Albert, 75005 Paris, France.

Unless otherwise stated, all scripture quotations
are from *The Good News Bible* (British-usage
edition), published by the Bible Societies and
Collins, © American Bible Society 1976;
reproduced by permission.

Printed by Redesign, London E2 9PB

ISBN 2-904-972-52-8

With gratitude to the Fourth World,
this courageous people from whom
I have received the Gospel.

ABOUT THE AUTHOR

Joseph Wresinski was born to an immigrant couple (a Polish father and a Spanish mother) in a working-class neighbourhood of Angers, France in 1917. He grew up in a family marked by social exclusion and extreme poverty. After gaining a primary school certificate, he became a pastry chef's apprentice at 13. In 1934, he joined the Young Christian Workers. Two years later, an elderly couple offered to cover the expenses for his admission to the seminary.

Enlisted in 1939, he was taken prisoner in the French capitulation. He managed to escape and returned to his studies in Soissons. Ordained in 1946, he was assigned to the parish of Tergnier as parish priest. In 1948, he joined the Mission of France. After a time at a sanatorium, he was made the curate of Dhuizel where he organised missions to preach about poverty in various regions of France.

In 1956, he was given the mission of working in the camp for the homeless in Noisy-le-Grand, just outside Paris. Together with the people of the camp, he founded the movement Aide à Toute Détresse, now called the International Movement ATD Fourth World. In 1961, he founded the Movement's Institute for Research on Poverty. As a result of his journeys and addresses, the Movement's projects soon spread to other European countries and to the United States.

Father Joseph Wresinski worked with many national and international organisations, participated in colloquia, served on a variety of commissions and founded a permanent volunteer corps within the Fourth World Movement. In 1978, he founded the Permanent Forum on Extreme Poverty, and the Movement's actions spread to the Third World. In 1979, Father Joseph was named a member of France's Economic and Social Council. He was the author of the "Report on Extreme Poverty and Economic and Social Insecurity", which the Council passed in 1987.

Today the International Movement ATD Fourth World includes more than 300 permanent volunteers, and is active in 116 countries on four continents. Both volunteers and members are men and women of all faiths, philosophies and social backgrounds who desire to join the poorest and the most rejected peoples in their struggle to build a better future for their children. They follow in the footsteps of Father Joseph, who fought all his life so that the voices of the poorest families would be heard and understood, so that exclusion would no longer be the fate of a part of humanity, and so that all people could have access to education, to knowledge, to modern skills, and, above all, to full participation in the life of the community.

Father Joseph died on February 14th, 1988. He is buried beside the chapel at the Movement's international centre in Méry-sur-Oise, France.

TABLE OF CONTENTS

Foreword by John Aloysius Ward,
    Archbishop of Cardiff   1

Introduction: The Gospel Read by the Poorest   5

I.   The Temptation in the Desert, or the
     Irrevocable Choice   16

II.   The Crowd, Always Bearing First Witness   42

III.   "... the Lame, the Blind, the Crippled,
     the Mute, and Many Others..."   66

IV.   "Lord, If You Are Willing, You Can
     Make Me Clean"   85

V.   "Nor Shall You Be Called Teacher..."   107

VI.   Gestures Which Restore Honour   129

VII.   The Salvation of the Poorest, a Scandal   142

VIII.   The Penitent Thief, a Companion
     for Eternity   166

IX.   Mary Magdalene, the Church's First Steps   176

X.   Architects of God's Justice   190

XI.   "Take Courage and Do Not Fear, It Is I"   212

XII.   Saint Joseph, the Believer of All Times   242

XIII.   Magnificat!   263

FOREWORD

A few years ago, shortly before his death, Father Joseph Wresinski visited Cardiff to speak with Church leaders. He introduced us to the Fourth World and to the Movement he had founded, to help us identify and minister to the truly poor in our immediate society.

He was a good teacher. The identification of those who know extreme poverty and economic and social insecurity was an eye-opener for us. Our pastoral experience had taught us much about poverty in Britain. Furthermore, our Churches had been made well aware of the needy in many parts of the so-called Third World. For us to have been ignorant of this poverty would have been culpable. Father Joseph, too, had given much of his life and ministry to reach out to the poor at home and abroad. But he spoke of another world—he chose to call it the Fourth World —where so much of its poverty is not so easily recognised or readily acknowledged. It is a world of people whose lives are blighted by inability to make use of opportunities to better their education, health, employment prospects, living conditions, family stability and advancement. The Fourth World is a fettered, often silent, world whose chains of blocked opportunities can only be broken with the help of those who recognise and acknowledge its existence.

Father Joseph and his Movement are important prophets on behalf of this Fourth World. This volume of Father Joseph's reflections will stir the conscience of any God-fearing person. To a Christian, he will come over as a prophet of the New Testament who brings to new life the Gospel of "the Least Brethren".

Father Joseph was a man of humble origins. When he spoke out on behalf of the poor, he spoke with his whole being: mind and heart and soul, his eyes and hands. Any emotion was measured; it was the Gospel language that took care that the Master's Voice could be heard. Joseph Wresinski wanted only that the loving compassion of Jesus of Nazareth came through. When he spoke to us in Cardiff, we knew we had met a rare human being. He had been shaped by the Gospel: the Master's life and mission; Gospel teaching and values. We met a man "at home" in the Gospel that made him a great servant of humanity. We were privileged to meet a powerful herald of the Gospel with a soul-searching gaze that echoed Jesus' plea for the forgotten poor and marginalised. We will never forget him; his visit was a moment of grace for us.

Father Joseph's work lives on. This book of his reflections is a great gift. May those who read it meet Father Joseph and be touched by this man of the Gospel. And may they, like the author, be "at home" in the Gospel.

John Aloysius Ward
Archbishop of Cardiff
May 1992

The Gospel Read by the Poorest

For many years now, I have felt I owed it to the Church to recall and tell others how I learned to recognise the dazzling unity of the Gospel. How were my eyes prepared to see its faultless consistency, the universality which, to me, makes it the Good News of all times? Through whom, in what way, did such grace befall me? I deeply wished to bear witness to this gift of God. Yet when the occasion arose, I hesitated. Indeed, many authors today commit their best efforts to inventing other words, other parables, translating the Gospel into something new. They set out to explore its history to the core, certainly not to change its spirit, but to update its language so that present generations may better

5

understand it. A necessary effort no doubt, since people seem to feel a need for it. But to what final purpose? Whose language needs updating, for the benefit of whom? For whom was the Gospel's language intended in the days of Jesus Christ? Can we be sure that it was the language of its time, within easy grasp of all in the fairly mixed Jewish society of that period? Could it be that our Lord had made a choice of terms, examples and gestures readily understood by some, while requiring more attentive listening on the part of others? Through our present efforts of translating His words, are we sure we comply with His plan?

These questions troubled me. For more than one reason, I hesitated to approach the Gospel as if it were a land of the past where a language was spoken which needed translation. Since my early childhood, my own path had been quite different. Approaching the Gospel, to me, had always been like returning to my native land. In the universe where I saw the Lord come and go, I felt at home, as in a very real and familiar setting. Growing up in a poverty-stricken family where we rarely ate to our heart's content, seeing my mother constantly humiliated because of her lack of means, I recognised among those who surrounded Jesus the faces and voices of my daily existence. Close to Jesus I saw poor people I knew but whom I did not meet when going to school or anywhere else outside our neighbourhood. I needed more translation in the better-off areas of my hometown than I did in the Gospel.

In my childhood I first met the Church through the men and women who represented it nearby: the parish priest, a saintly man who later became my bishop, the good sisters of the Holy Shepherd where I served mass when I was barely five. I have already written about this Church, which was poor, often slandered in those days, and which bore no trace of haughtiness. It respected my mother in her extreme misery, in ways she was not always respected by her neighbours nor, to be sure, by the well-to-do families who employed her as a charwoman. Prayer, trust in God the Father, I learned from my mother sitting motionless, late at night, in the kitchen which was our only room, silently asking the Lord for solutions that surely must have been in the nature of miracles, considering the depth of our poverty. Did she perhaps pray only for help to endure the problems to which there were no solutions? Did she perhaps ask God for the strength to make the best of things, seeing that "there is always someone poorer than we are," as she used to say? At any rate, this is how I learned to know the Church, humble and respecting the humble. God, beyond any doubt, was a Father who could understand and help. Assistance, turning up at moments of extreme emergency, even if I had been the one to find it, made me believe in a God who would not abandon my mother. Such were the beginnings of my religious education. For the child in poverty which I was, the Church of the poor was a reality, long before Vatican II. To the Gospel as a message of the poor, to the Gospel *for* the poorest, I found my way more gradually. That Gospel was taught to me by the very poor who continued to surround me as the years went by.

Housed in a mere hovel, my family was always in

danger of being broken up, my mother being urged to let us children be placed in an orphanage. I saw my mother ever-dependent on charity and therefore never free to do as she pleased. We lived on the borderline between an area notorious for its poverty and a working-class neighbourhood. Thus, I gradually discovered what must have been the crowds gathering around Jesus, what His words must have meant to different kinds of people. The woman of Samaria, the woman of Canaan, the penitent thief, the publican at the back of the temple, the old woman making such a fuss over a retrieved drachma—they all seemed so familiar to me. The crowd of the humble, the most wretched lagging in its wake, always late, ever pushing their way and inconveniencing all, people displaying their sores, their infirmities, their sufferings, . . . they were no surprise to me. I always felt I had already met them, and indeed I had! The very poor in downtown Angers, now merging with the crowd, now rejected and surging back to their shanties, their garrets, their dark and squalid tenements, they were not really different. Their language and behaviour were the same. Thanks to them, I learned to feel at home in the Gospel. This closeness across time and space came from the similarity of the social condition of the poor and the poorest, now and in those days long past. Then, as now, the real difference was between the very poor and the well-off. The former could understand and bounce with joy at the words of Jesus. The latter were often completely at sea. They would criticise His teachings and question His miracles, refusing to listen and to believe as the poor never would.

8

It had been my extraordinary fortune to get acquainted at a very early age with those who could grasp miracles as no one else could. I lived among families capable of understanding how inconceivable, unwonted and unprecedented Christ's choice in favour of the poorest really was. I did not need to stretch my imagination to visualise the people to whom our Lord so persistently turned His eyes and directed His steps. The lame and the blind, those who wept of shame, those who rushed out to follow Jesus with no thought of taking supplies for the road, I knew them all. It is to them that I owe the Gospel. They taught me neither its historical and theological intricacies nor a detailed exegesis, satisfactory to the mind. I owe to these ill-treated people of my own time, whom misery had sometimes disfigured beyond recognition, the feeling of being permanently within the Gospel, the Lord always ahead, just around the next corner, His loved ones close to me, His spirit everywhere and a miracle always about to happen. Conversion, salvation were present behind the tears of a mother or the anxiety of a man who would say to me, "Father, I can't take it any longer. . . ." I deeply believe that the poorest were in the days of Jesus, and have remained through the ages, the reality of the Gospel present in everyday life. They do not necessarily master its more intellectual interpretations, but they sense right away its essential meaning and its basic truth. By virtue of their very misery, they have the intuition that the plan of God is the only one possible, whereas others ask themselves a thousand questions: "Can this truly be what Jesus meant?" The very poor are better able to guide us toward contemplation and meditation than our more privileged fellow human beings. They silence our criticism and cold reasoning, making room for the mystery of love, of which the Gospel has remained the most perfect living history of our time. They show us how this history remains true to itself, as real today as it was then.

Only much later did I realise that a misunderstanding could arise on this point, due to a misapprehension about the social position we must ascribe to Jesus. What station in life did He choose? In the personality and daily existence of what man was He born and molded? To what extent did He really become a man of that condition? Did He, the Son of God, choose only to stand on the side of the humble for the sake of a strategy or a pedagogical purpose? Or did He really become a man in poverty Himself, virtually modelled as a man in poverty "in all things but sin"? And if He chose to be truly poor rather than only declaring Himself on the side of the poor, how deep was His poverty? Was Jesus just one among the great many poor of those days, one among a poor and oppressed people, son of an artisan, secure in His humble community? Many see Him as such. Yet, His birth and.death as an outcast, His entire existence and teaching may call for a more subtle identification.

Was He not in fact the son of a menial labourer who did the rough carpentry that a peasant population would not do itself? Was not His father a lowly labourer so obviously poor that at the inn of Bethlehem they could direct him without qualms to a cave in the nearby hills? Jesus came into the world as did only the children of bandits and shepherds, a backward and most asocial population in the eyes of a people which had turned to a sedentary life, cultivating its fields in an orderly fashion. To them, not only theft but trades liable to incite to theft—such as herding cattle for rich proprietors—were classified impure. And this child Jesus set out in life as the son of wanderers, His parents fleeing to the Negev where foreigners were doomed to unemployment unless they accepted tasks reserved for slaves. When they returned at last to their land, Joseph had to seek work in a much impoverished community, despised for its deprivation and lack of culture. What did it mean to be a carpenter among a people deprived of their fields by the Romans and whose unemployed had to sit by the wayside, waiting for a landowner to hire them for a few hours? In the town of Nazareth, getting poorer by the day, what kind of a clientele could an artisan like Joseph have? Jesus was a Jew, but what kind of Jew? Jesus of the House of David, to be sure, but also Jesus the Galilean, son of a people suspected of ritual impurity, sometimes rebellious and largely invaded by uncircumcised pagans. Jesus of the land of Galilee which the priests and the Pharisees of Jerusalem shunned for its ignorance and its ill repute. Jesus, one among the poorest in this rejected land, who even in His youth must have been acquainted with ungodly Greeks.

God evidently had not shaped a play nor organised a "role play" as do today's psychologists. Besides, how could we ever surmise that the Lord would resort to a mere "mise-en-scène" for the edification of humanity? Could we deny that God in His love went all the way, bringing His Son into the world as the lowest among the low? A friend of mine recently asserted that "in the days of Jesus there were no excluded among the people." Does such a claim represent a solid analysis of the life of the Son of God made man? Does it show even a minimum of understanding of the states of poverty and oppression which sooner or later drive their victims to oppress in their turn the weakest among them?

If it be true that God loved humanity to the very end, if this was no mere pretence but true fulfilment of His commitment to humanity, then the language and gestures of Christ were those of the poorest. Then all He said and did was perfectly comprehensible to them. Better still: for their part, they could talk to Him, answer Him in their own words. They could even argue with Him, holding their own, but not as would the rich, setting traps for Him. They could challenge Him as they would someone they expected to say what they longed to hear, to confirm their hopes. In the Gospel, Jesus speaks and acts as a man totally at ease among the most rejected, and they in turn talk back to Him and behave without affectation. Those who are close to the poorest today can bear witness to this. The modes of speech and behaviour we meet in the Gospel have remained perfectly intelligible to the poorest throughout the centuries.

In this book, we shall try to deal with the everyday life and the genuine kinship of Jesus with the poorest, with how they spoke to Him and what He meant to them. We shall also try to understand the kinship of the very poor today with those close to

Jesus; a kinship which renders superfluous all mediation, all translation or transposition. As I said, thanks to the poorest of my own time, the Gospel has become to me much more than a text to read; a land where I can go and meet with men and women familiar in speech and gestures and ever worthy of love. Because I love the families mutilated by extreme poverty who surround me, I am ever eager to join those who jostled Jesus Christ. As a matter of course, they are equally precious, equally moving to my heart. To meditate on Jesus and to love Him as He appears in the Gospel (I do not dare say: to keep company with Him), to associate with those for whom He had such limitless mercy, represents an immeasurable grace. Only the very poor can obtain it for their more privileged fellow people. In the Gospel I find my mother and my former neighbours in the Rue Saint Jacques, as I find those countless families so poor and despised whom I came to know later, all along the years of my priesthood. Only to this Gospel where the poor come and go can I bear witness. It is a Gospel full of bittersweet encounters. I know of no other and I can know this one only through the meditation and love the poorest taught me. Mine is a knowledge through the eyes of the heart, as Saint Paul puts it. The poor have no other way to know.

The testimony I wish to bear cannot be but an act of grace, as have been other testimonies published before mine. My way of reading the Gospel, the reading of the very poor, will not contradict theirs. All sincere efforts to grasp the very essence of the Gospel are destined to meet and to complement one

13

another for the Lord, who conversed as a man in dire poverty with the poor and the poorest, spoke with the very same tenderness to the well-off, the rich and even the most wealthy. He addressed the learned and the mighty as well as those who between the rich and the poor may figure as the "common people." He excluded none, spoke to all, whether they were of good will, indifferent or hostile. It is true that He demanded from some a more considerable effort to understand what He so readily revealed to others. He expected those who held high rank, knowledge and power to exert themselves to discern what He directly disclosed to the small and the humble. This remains true up to this very day and we shall try to look at it through the eyes of the poorest of our own time. The main point to keep in mind is that Christ, while demanding different efforts from people in different conditions, showed equal love for all. In confronting the affluent with greater demands, He honours them. They are as much concerned and He loves them as deeply as He does the humble. When reading the Gospel with the eyes of the poorest, we in fact discover His love in its full splendour.

Proceeding this way, we shall finally become aware that achieving the Kingdom of God is not easier for the poor, even if they are quicker to understand the Good News. The very poor themselves agree that peace, unity, love among all people must be bought at a certain price, though the cost may vary according to each person's means. They ask for no privilege on this account. They do not think their salvation should be free of charge. They request forgiveness and they desire to take part in the common effort. We shall try

14

to clarify this too. What teaching, what guidelines and demands do the poor draw from the Gospel, for themselves as well as for all humanity?

Explore and experience the Gospel, meditate on it as the poor taught me to do, by all means! But let us never forget that their intimacy with Jesus Christ will remain a mystery forever. A mystery for which no pen can account.

CHAPTER ONE

The Temptation in the Desert, or the Irrevocable Choice

A person born in a poverty-stricken family, in a milieu so poor as to suffer constant anxiety and humiliation, cannot wish to remain in that condition. Neither the feeling of belonging there, nor the conviction that he owes solidarity to his own in their struggle for a better life can make him accept being held in contempt. It would be against his nature and his very calling as a human being. Poverty, material deprivation, oppression inflicted by those who have power are hard to bear. What is truly insufferable, however, is being despised and continuously reminded that one is an inferior and utterly useless being. Fourth World families bring this home to us day by day. Being treated as a person without dignity

16

even by one's own is virtually intolerable. "People treat us like nobodies. . . . Are we dogs, to be kicked around as we are at the Town Hall?"

This is where the difference lies between poverty and misery. A person in misery suffers an unbearable situation, being considered negligible or, worse, a harmful being who should never have been born, while deep inside he still knows he is a person. To long for dignity, to dream of being someone and yet to be denied this even by those hardly better off than oneself: the neighbours, the grocer, the postman, . . . that is misery. And that is what makes the difference between poverty and exclusion.

I had to learn this early in life, seeing people hold one another off when they had everything to gain by joining forces. I noticed the ambiguity of the relations between my mother and the lady next door, even more forsaken and who had taken to drinking. I witnessed violence in the St. Nicholas neighbourhood nearby. Families, all equally deprived, scorned one another: "I am not like them, they are a pack of thieves, I don't even know them. . . . Just look at them neglecting their children!" The children, of course, would be allowed to share the evening meal, as my mother did with the boy of the lady next door, provided we had food to share. But between such small gestures and declaring to be friends, seeking out the company of others in the name of neighbourliness or of one's sharing the same living conditions, there was an almost impassable barrier, as if deciding in favour of those even poorer than oneself meant denying oneself, renouncing one's own dignity.

This lesson learnt day by day prompts me to return unceasingly, always with fear, but also with ever the same wonder, to Jesus tempted in the desert. The event and the mystery it carries seem too sacred for our human eyes to behold. Still, I cannot resist the compulsion to remain in their presence. The destiny of the Son of God in this world, the liberation of the poorest and therefore of all humanity are at stake there, once and for all. The Evangelist Matthew makes us witness the incredible in just a few sentences, startling by their very restraint:

Then the Spirit led Jesus into the desert
to be tempted by the Devil.
After spending forty days
and forty nights without food, Jesus was hungry.
Then the Devil came to Him and said,
"If You are God's Son,
order these stones to turn into bread."
But Jesus answered,
"The scripture says,
'Man cannot live on bread alone,
but needs every word that God speaks.'"
Then the Devil took Jesus to Jerusalem,
the Holy City,
set Him on the highest point of the temple
and said to Him:
"If You are God's Son,
Throw Yourself down, for the Scripture says:
'God will give orders to His angels about You;
they will hold you up in their hands,
so that not even Your feet
will be hurt on the stones.'"

Jesus answered,
"But the Scripture also says,
'Do not put the Lord your God to the test.'"
Then the Devil took Jesus
to a very high mountain
and showed Him all the kingdoms of the world
in all their greatness.
"All this I will give you," the Devil said,
"if you kneel down and worship me."
Then Jesus answered,
"Go away, Satan!
The Scripture says,
'Worship the Lord your God
and serve only Him.'"
Then the Devil left Jesus;
and angels came and helped Him.

(Matthew 4, 1-11)

Can we be anything but bewildered when we imagine the complete reversal Jesus brings about in the course of the world's history? From this moment, nothing will ever be the same again, everything becomes equally possible to all, be they rich, poor or excluded. Fear, diffidence and infinite gratitude mingle in my heart because of all I have learnt from the poor in my youth and ever since.

Even before the temptation, we knew God's will that His Son be made a man among the most humble. In Bethlehem, it is God who speaks. Obviously not any couple arriving at the inn unexpectedly would have been shunted off to a cave, even in an exceptional peak period. Not any mother would have been called upon to bring her first son into the world in a

19

place where only bandits' and shepherds' children and lambs were born. The Holy Virgin was referred there because it was God's will that His Son be born among these migrant people who did not take part in religious rites and who were always under suspicion, considered impure because of their trade and whose testimony was not valid in court. Through these shepherds rarely seen at the Temple, God addresses Himself to the world. Even as He speaks to the world today, reminding us of His plan through these families snubbed in court: "Hold your tongue! . . . How can you expect to be taken seriously, living as you do in a broken truck and scavenging for a livelihood?" God also speaks to us through the Burniers, this young couple, shelterless and out of work in the Paris area, to whom the local authorities in the depth of winter offer nothing but a tarpaulin. At the same time, in that same municipality, the Meuniers are allotted a state-subsidised apartment because the father, a qualified welder, offers the required guarantee that he will pay the rent. In that winter of 1983, a boy is born to the Burniers in their tent, the family lacking the means to get to the hospital when the hour has come.

Bethlehem and later, Nazareth, were the word of God Himself choosing the family of a manual worker, with neither prestige nor security, be it only the security that the child would survive. Jesus will live His childhood on the brink of misery. He will have the time to really learn what extreme poverty means, getting to know it inside out, as it were. He will experience the atmosphere in a family forced to move from place to place, having to beg for work in its land of exile. He will discover the existence of the carpenter come home, having lost his place in the community as well as his skill in a trade he has not practised for years. Jesus will know what it means to live in a home even poorer than most in an altogether poverty-stricken milieu. In this land of Galilee, generally shunned by the authorities in Jerusalem, He will live at the bottom of the social scale, there where in all regions and cultures, at all times, people of uncertain identity, foreigners and travelling people of all sorts, one way or another suspected of impurity, come to mingle with the landless and menial labourers.

It is one thing to be poor and live in more or less severe material deprivation within a community itself reduced to harsh austerity; being even poorer than most, less safely established, looked down upon or even suspected is still different. It seems that God has willed that Jesus would know this, that even very young He would meet the victims of extreme poverty, learning the burden of wretchedness, coarseness, awkwardness and despair they carry deep inside. Misery and exclusion make people neither kind nor attractive. They do not teach them elegant language, nor bearing, nor self-confidence. They break bodies and crush souls, leaving people totally dependent on the varying good will of others, never sure where they stand, or what to expect from others or even from themselves. Jesus will know the difference between poverty and sheer misery. And in His home, He will learn what tremendous effort it takes to remain a family despite the toll of vagrancy, exclusion and humiliation. He will grow up with parents known to be just, because they resist the effects of isolation, impoverishment, insecurity and contempt to remain true to the plans of God.

It is this very Jesus, close to the extremely poor for having known and experienced their sorrows, whom we are going to meet again in the desert at the scene of the Temptation. Sooner or later temptation was bound to come. Eventually the Son must, in His turn and of His own free will, choose the design conceived by His Father. And in order to pledge total obedience, He must choose with full knowledge of the facts.

Such was Christ's choice, one that seems almost unbelievable and unacceptable even to many Christians today. The Lord knew the condition He chose. The hour of the Temptation was not only the moment in which to choose the situation He would embrace in the world: it was the hour in which Jesus deliberately chose the men and women who had to bear that situation. Among the crowd of the poor, Jesus' preference would go to those whom no one but He would choose, the crippled, the lepers, the men of ill repute, the prostitutes, the lame, all those whom the poor themselves tend to ignore and who therefore are the most wretched and vulnerable. Of this we are also aware, day by day, in all parts of the world, in all cultures. No need to update the illustrations, the parables. They apply to all ages.

For who is unhappier than a man who cannot even call himself a worker and who therefore is neither solicited nor defended by any form of worker solidarity? As a menial worker employed on isolated, servile and occasional jobs, he is just good enough to sweep, unload or cart for an employer who is himself lagging behind the economic progress of his time. Today, he is chronically unemployed even before having experienced a regular career. Who could be more wretched than his wife, who is not legally married to him and must hide her pregnancy from the social worker, forsaking prenatal care for fear of losing custody of her baby? Who is unhappier than her eldest son who goes to school and hears his classmates say, "Beat it, you stink! Anyway, my mother told me not to play with you because you have lice!"

Even today the crippled are still on the rutted paths, the untouchables linger in the streets at night, waiting for the Salvation Army or Emmaüs van to pass, delivering soup and yoghurt, just as the repudiated women, the widows accused of witchcraft, the orphans who represent excess mouths to feed in a draught-ridden village, remain on the rutted paths or sheltered under an old tin roof. Lepers are still among us throughout the world. Cared for and cured as they could not be in the days of Jesus, the poorest among them yet remain out of reach or shut up in desolate confinement, chased out of their communities, or even chained to trees when no care is available. In the chapters ahead we shall meet many of these very poorest chosen by the Lord and whom He knew so well. We can easily recognise them amongst us, even now.

Could there be any doubt that Jesus Christ both chose their condition and chose them? Some pretend that exclusion did not exist at the time. Exclusion, they say, is a modern phenomenon, typical of Western societies. This assertion does considerable harm to the poorest who are virtually excluded from their communities in developing countries. It allows us to ignore their sorrow for not being counted among the poor for whom improvement is in store. Ignoring their suffering, we also overlook the fact that they have a privileged place in the Kingdom.

By our legitimate desire to imagine solidarity among the poor, do we not furthermore risk wronging Christ Himself? He never ceased to dispel our dream, drawing from obscurity those whom His people had rejected. Outcasts did exist and the Gospel tells us of Jesus' very special tenderness for them. If they existed then as they do now, would it not mean offending the Lord if we pretended that He went only halfway in His incarnation? God had not gone halfway when placing His son in a manger. When the time came to choose perfect obedience to His Father, could Jesus' answers have contained any reservations? Would the Lord have fixed limits to His love, deciding to go to a certain depth, but not to the core of the human condition? By virtue of its very sobriety, Matthew's text does not seem to allow for such an interpretation.

"If You are God's Son, order these stones to turn into bread" (Matthew 4,3). Jesus, famished Himself, brother of the hungry, refuses to turn even the smallest stone into bread. He does not refuse "a certain power." He renounces all economic power in this world. Only forty days ago, a voice from Heaven revealed, "This is my own dear Son, with whom I am pleased." (Matthew 3, 17) Will Jesus, immersed in poverty for thirty years, draw any material advantage from His Father's acknowledgement? "Man cannot live on bread alone, but needs every word that God speaks." Jesus Himself is the word of God. In the face of this reality, the question whether stones will be turned into bread loses its relevance and needs no longer be asked.

The devil then offers political power, worldly glory and might in another form. "Throw Yourself down, for the Scripture says, 'God will give orders to His angels about You . . . '" Does Jesus, brother of the most humble, think of getting even with the world? "Do not put the Lord your God to the test." Christ cannot mistake any personal interest for the plan of God. In fact, Jesus says: There can be for me no other interests but those of my Father.

The devil finally takes Him to the high mountain to show Him the world's kingdoms. "All this I will give You, if You kneel down and worship me." Here is absolute political power, offered to the man of Galilee so profoundly aware of political extortion and oppression. He is in a position to measure the instant relief which political power entrusted to His hands could bring. Still, "Go away, Satan! The Scripture says, 'Worship the Lord your God and serve only Him.'" Does not the "go away!" express an unconditional and irrevocable choice? Does Jesus not clearly assert His will to remain close to those who will not only bring Him neither prestige nor fame, but on the contrary will immerse Him in ignominy? The very poorest of yesterday, like those of today, not only can give Him no support whatsoever; they are even going to draw increasing suspicion upon Him. Worse still, they will be induced to deny Him, and Christ knows this. He knows His own well enough to realise how misery can compel men and women to betray the only ones who could be their friends.

How could we think that Jesus would keep for Himself even the smallest shred of security? In the face of His threefold unequivocal renunciation of all power, would not the slightest doubt on our part mean an insult? The only explanation I can find for our cautious interpretations and our reluctance to accept the magnitude of His sacrifice is our own fear of seeing Him choose absolute vulnerability and of having to follow Him even that far. Just as only our fear of our most disfigured fellow men and women can explain our reticence to admit that in choosing irremediable weakness, Christ also chose them personally. To choose the condition without choosing the victims would still have been a manner of stopping halfway, claiming an exclusive situation and repute: I shall live their condition on my own, I will not share it with them. That would have been a way to make a name for Himself by using His own power of decision. Then Jesus would have escaped after all that most humiliating of all conditions of having no choice and being doomed to bear with the disgrace heaped on the most defamed around Him. This is what families crowded into very poor housing settlements teach us day by day. Being herded together, they have no chance whatsoever to ward off the shame that each family on its own might still have avoided. It was not by chance that Christ, later on, so often compromised Himself with the most forsaken among this people in poverty.

But how can we lift our eyes on Christ who freely makes this choice and not feel bewildered? Even the very poor themselves would have been unable to choose such an option. As for me, I have been marked and my faith in Jesus' divinity has been sealed, not so much by His miracles or His doctrine, as by the fact that He dared what no other would dare, ever before or ever after. He went beyond that freely chosen poverty, which remains a privilege, to identify Himself fully with those who were then and are now at the bottom of the social scale: the outcast lepers, the irremediably disabled, the forsaken paralytics, the possessed and those held to be possessed and therefore banned to living in caves, the spurned prostitutes — in a word, all those who were then and are now held to be marginal. I feel that this is how Jesus never ceased to reveal Himself as the Son of God, turning the utterly rejected into the leaven in the dough, into the first builders of the Kingdom. "Sinners and prostitutes have precedence over you." And we well know how sin, impurity and extreme poverty were intertwined, how they hung together in the existence of the Jewish people in those days. The belief that those who crossed the law were cursed bred contempt and not only religious, but also social and economic discrimination. A good part of the people therefore were condemned to poverty, while the most scorned were totally excluded, often irrevocably branded as impure from one generation to another. Is it not in identifying Himself with them that Jesus truly shows His divine nature? The pagans, He says, and all those you put on the same footing, expelling them from the Temple because of their ignorance, will be the ones to lead the way.

I feel that at the hour of temptation, Jesus made the choice which proclaimed His divinity, an all the more stunning choice as He knew what and whom He chose, as well as what He was giving up. His decision was made in full knowledge of the facts, since He possessed the double experience both of misery and of the might and the glory which are its opposite.

Jesus refused to be mighty, while He knew He could be. He also knew the joy and pride one draws from giving to neighbours what one needs for one-self. The lives of the very poor are filled with gestures like this. They give or lend because they experience the intolerable deprivation of basic necessities themselves and cannot accept it either for themselves or for others. But they also give because giving offers the purest form of gratification, the one of feeling more fully human. To convince ourselves of this, we need but look at some of these seemingly insane gestures like passing on food to a neighbour when there isn't even enough for one's own evening meal, giving a bank note to the postman or the fireman for their annual fundraising, while the family purse cannot afford shoes for the children. The very poor often give what they do not have. They take the bread from their own mouths, as my mother used to say. She did so for her own children, but also for the boy whose mother had taken to drinking, for the widow further down the street whom no one would help, and whose body was found one day, two weeks after she had died of starvation.

Turning stones into bread, what blessing! Being able to feed people to satiety, what temptation for a man in poverty! Jesus knows and yet renounces. True, the time will come for Him to do miracles and multiply bread. But these miracles will then confirm precisely that which the tempter wanted to see denied. They will tell the poor that Christ is one of them. These gestures of Jesus have always enchanted me. They clearly show how well Jesus knew by what signs the very poor would be able to recognise His life and message, to grasp what none could have explained to them in words, namely that He knew and loved them. These miracles, expressing all Jesus' intimacy and collusion with the poor and the poorest, always have been a message of love, never an assumption of power.

Nor did Jesus accept to make use of His knowledge to gain worldly power. Yet He realised what it meant to be heeded and admired for one's learning. Had He not surprised even the most highly qualified scholars at the Temple, He the young man of Galilee, despised for its ignorance? Again, what revenge on the world, what satisfaction and security to be able to teach and inspire admiration and respect, rather than indignation, fear and hatred! God had endowed His Son with the means to secure all knowledge. He had given Him the possibility of realising what power it could earn. Here again, Jesus knew and yet renounced.

In short, Jesus knew all that the excluded and all the poor among His people were thirsting for, and He was aware He could give it to them. He could reshape society and procure material security for all. He could establish a new social order, offer new techniques to alleviate daily toil and enhance creativity. He could dismantle existing structures to make room for new ones — all providing, of course, that He played into the hands of worldly systems. Paradoxically, He was offered all possibilities, on the condition that He submit His divine nature to worldly rules. This was in fact what the tempter proposed and if his proposal had not contained real possibilities, there would have been no temptation. The devil was right when he said: It is in Your power to obtain honour, to win the attributes of a king, to overcome Your enemies; Your eloquence is sufficiently captivating to dazzle the crowds, and they but wait to follow You. You have nothing to fear, You cannot fail nor be overthrown. Provided You play by my rules, those of the strength of weapons, police forces and repression. . . . Providing You worship me.

No doubt Satan's proposal is one of the issues that has given Christians, Christian fighters for all kinds of human causes, and the Church generally, more than they bargained for. We learn that to become a politician fighting for justice or a statesman earning a name that will make history, we shall have to compromise one way or another with the very evil we set out to defeat. After a temporary easing of the burden of the oppressed, after a fleeting surge of the people's enthusiasm, will come the time to worship Satan, the time of bloodshed and renewed inferno, of the restoration of supremacy and privileges for some and of muzzling and oppression of the others. Then slander, hatred, corruption and subversion will inevitably return. . . .

The devil laid his cards on the table before Jesus and the Gospel does as much before us, offering the most important political lesson of all time. The kingdom founded on worldly power will be an illusion for those who suffer. It may at first bring bread and a burst of exhilaration. But very soon, humanity will be back in the anti-kingdom which furthers the opposite of justice, brotherhood and truth. Christ could not have accepted this. The Temptation tells us that following the paths of God means having no recourse other than Him, being as totally dependent on Him as are the excluded. We shall learn no more for the time being. The Gospel invites us to bow before Christ who renounces all worldly power, without yet knowing where He will lead us. Too much impatience to know more might make us miss the present crucial encounter. We sense that the affairs of the Father can never again be merged with those of the world, as Satan would have it; but for the time being, it is essential that we do not yet seek to understand where this will lead us. First, we must simply contemplate Christ as He announces His baffling choice. Indeed, I feel that the Gospel at this juncture calls for a halt and a time of silence to come closer to the personality of Jesus.

This is certainly the way the very poor of our day see it. Jesus choosing to be as vulnerable as they are, astonishes but also enchants them and fills them with joy. For them, this is a moment to experience intensely and an event to return to often in order to make it one's own. For many, it means a feast, the sudden fulfilment of an obscure expectation. Fourth World families teach me that contemplation of Christ which asks for no understanding of what is to follow. In fact, we would not comprehend all that is to come, if we did not pause in the desert.

Is it not because we allow ourselves so little time for meditation that we can so easily be mistaken about the further events in the Gospel as well as about the guidelines we draw from them? Jesus, it is said, abandoned the poor to the world's injustice; the Kingdom would come some other day. Others, on the contrary, compare Jesus to revolutionaries as the world knows them, who place the cause of the poor in the setting of a struggle *against* other people, their freedom to be obtained through the muzzle of a gun. These are all conclusions from which meditation on the Temptation in the desert can preserve us. Christ does not postpone the liberation of the poor or the salvation of humanity to some later time. Nor does the Gospel allow us to reduce Christ to a mere "leader," or worse, to a symbol of an earthly leader. The Lord makes such conjectures pointless; He raises action to other heights, offering other arms. All must be revised in the light of the definite option chosen at the hour of confrontation with Satan.

Later, Jesus will say, "I am with you always, to the very end of time." I shall be on earth, you will have only to open your eyes to see me, you will never need to imagine me. But how will Jesus be among us, in whom shall we recognise Him? Through the temptation in the desert, He tells us once and for all; He leaves His people in no uncertainty. I shall be with you in the person of the poorest, the most humiliated, the most neglected. I shall remain abandoned as they are, consigned to injustice without appeal. The person, the family ignored even by the just and the defenders of human rights, they will be me. . . .

Jesus says, "I am with you." But He also says, "You are with me." All of you who make the choice I did in the desert, on the summit of the Temple, on the mountain peak, every time you could use power to heighten your prestige and yet you renounce it to remain with the humblest so that they may free themselves, you will be with me. Every time you give up a privilege, a possession, every time you risk losing status and security so that the poorest may stand upright, you follow me. God will offer you the choice as He did me. You will be free to accept or refuse.

Indeed, the Temptation tells us that Christ will save the world not only by His birth and His crucifixion as a man in poverty, unjustly treated as a criminal; Jesus Christ saves the world by His free choice of the destiny of an outcast and by compromising Himself with the excluded. His sacrifice is perfect because He has truly willed it. Saint Francis of Assisi may well have been the one who grasped this most fully and who best identified himself with Jesus all at once made man and Son of God, poor and crucified. Over the centuries, this identification will be the main cause of anxiety to the Church, constantly faced with this temptation herself. How could she avoid faltering now and then? At times, the Church may lose her sense of the urgency of identifying with the very poorest. Sometimes the excluded themselves will come to remind the Church of her neglect, pilfering her possessions, burning down her buildings, as if in a blind and desperate protest against having been abandoned. The Church's times of strength will be when she will be brought back to the foot of the social scale, to the foot of the cross. Her times of strength will be when she will not only find herself one with the most vulnerable but also let it be known that they are her very core; when she will accept being lost to the world, in order to gain the world for the poor. These will be times when the Church relives the Temptation in the desert and, following the Lord, refuses worldly power in order to free all people.

The Church, Christians and all humanity will necessarily relive this Temptation, which was so crucial a moment in Jesus' life. Each one of us must face it in his own way, depending no doubt on his situation. But the confrontation is unavoidable and may present itself more than once. The poor and even the poorest will be faced with it. A priest, born poor and bent on remaining close to his own, will not escape it. It is by having faced the experience so regularly myself, all through my life as a worker and then as a priest, that I am so often brought back to the Lord at the hour of His decisive choice. I always return there with the same fear and humility, and I am no different in that from so many other priests, workers and Christians confronted with present-day injustice. Who among us is not tempted one day or another to become a leading trade unionist or politician, to use a gift of eloquence, a talent for captivating one's comrades, a capacity for analysis, to create oneself a position and obtain personal power in the name of justice?

34

I have never forgotten the years when, as a young curate among the railway workers in Tergnier, I joined their strikes. I questioned the women who remained on their doorsteps in the housing settlements: "Why are you not with your husbands, you who are first and foremost concerned by their struggle for an honourable life?" I remember emptying the parish shelves I had taken such pains to fill with a stock of food for the children's summer vacation. I handed over the rice, sugar and noodles to the families of the strikers. Then came the unpleasant surprise that those who had helped me prepare the children's vacation refused to replace these foodstuffs which in their eyes I had unwisely distributed to families on strike.

How could I admit that my own parishioners would not feel concerned but refused to take a stand in such struggles? Was it not their very vocation to want to contribute to a more just society where structures would consequently be changed? I still believe this. But in the course of these first experiences as a curate among workers in full struggle, I learned that by joining the strikers, in making their wives participate, I unwittingly moved away from the most downtrodden. Unskilled, with no real profession in hand and by far the most deprived, they were employed in the least rewarding, least regular and least paid jobs with Jappy or at Bautor. The few gains achieved by the striking railway workers, of course, did not apply to them. They did not belong to the same category of workers and their situation became even worse. Without realising it at the time, I was prompted to spend more and more time with them and their families, pained and humiliated as they were to see themselves ignored or not considered worth fighting for. The relations between the railway workers and the unskilled workers at Jappy did not improve this way.

Here is an apparently ordinary occurrence, a circumstantial experience for a priest who normally ever since his seminary days has tried to be present first in the most deprived urban areas. But to me it was a real lesson. I had plunged into the struggle, found my place and a personal satisfaction there, and as a result, I was already no longer quite on the side of the poorest. I also learned to understand better, and to love truly, many trade unionists of the lowest grade who refused promotions in their workplace because this would have separated them from their unskilled companions whose working conditions were the hardest. I profoundly believe that they should serve as a model in our present-day struggles on behalf of those we call the "new poor." The cause of these redundant workers, laid off since the economic recession of the '70s, obviously deserves vigorous support. Can we, however, take sides with these workers, while overlooking those who, unskilled and underemployed for much longer, have no chance whatsoever to participate in modernised economic structures tomorrow? To allow ourselves to be upset in our plans, to draw prejudice upon the efficiency of the general struggle of all workers, by giving priority to the poorest in all our battles: this is what Christ's answer to the tempter meant.

Of course, the temptation is not only to choose our companions among the stronger or to fail to make sure who will benefit by our efforts. I have had to learn many other lessons myself. I have often been uncertain about where I stood with regard to Jesus' own intransigence in the face of temptation. For even when one has chosen to be true to the poorest, one still has to decide the ways and means of one's combat. Day after day, that question remains. For one cannot set out to live among the very poor, keeping one's hands folded or sharing only their sorrows. To be with the poorest, to be one of them, means first of all to share their hopes and all they invent, and undertake to live in dignity and to free themselves from excessive deprivation. Choosing the excluded means choosing a struggle which will of necessity concern the means for daily living: food, housing, social benefits and assistance. To stand aloof from that struggle would mean that we remain absent from the existence and expectations of the families.

Jesus Himself did not remain an outsider to that daily struggle. He well and truly intervened in the lives of His people, but in so doing He never betrayed His answer to Satan: "Man does not live by bread alone. . . . You shall not tempt the Lord your God. . . . You shall worship Him only." I have had to keep repeating that to myself more and more often, as the ATD Fourth World Movement, founded with families in extreme poverty, grew. In becoming a member of the French Economic and Social Council, in meeting heads of state regularly, in addressing important United Nations meetings, in obtaining public aid from the European Economic Community or the Council of Europe, I had my place — be it ever so modest — in public life. Was I then still true to the choice of Jesus? Fourth World families are my people. I cannot imagine life without them. But am I still one with them, as the Gospel demands? Am I the voice of my people who suffer and hope, or have I become a personality on my own account? Is the prestige I achieved — if any — *their* prestige, *their* dignity recognised at last?

Most important of all: do the families find in me what I propose to *them*, namely to be always prepared to renounce benefits and status gained, in order to seek out people even more wretched and forsaken? Am I still capable myself, as was Christ, of renouncing every form of power or worldly system? Have I remained free to discover, love and act unreservedly among those who, because of excessive misery and solitude, remain outside all structures, including those of the ATD Fourth World Movement? Can families see this to be true by the way I live? Can they realise that my homilies, my manner of speech in their meetings, are not my own but are dictated by the Spirit which directs my daily existence? Can they ascertain that whatever God entrusted me with for their service actually serves the most rejected among them first, even at the risk of disappointing the others? Am I still one of them, always aware that I am nothing and can do nothing without them?

Like others who are committed to a cause, I am tempted to measure my efficiency by the fervour of the militants who converge around me, by the participation of the families at our "People's Universities," where they practise reflecting on important matters and expressing common thinking together. I should in fact measure my impact by what happens in people's hearts, by their assessment of me as a priest, by their willingness to be guided by the Spirit within them, whether or not they be Christians. I remember a private audience the Holy Father granted a delegation of eighty young people of the Fourth World who came from four different continents. We were but a few adults accompanying them and we might easily have been tempted to step in the lime-light ourselves, paying our respects to John Paul II. But we stayed behind, for this was the time of a face to face meeting between the Pope and the very poorest among young people throughout the world. It was *their* feast, not ours. While mounting the stairs at Castel Gondolfo, I said to myself, as on so many other occasions, "This is not your doing, it is the work of the Holy Spirit." I kept on thanking God for these youngsters, for their fathers always out of work, for their mothers who went hungry so that their children might eat. I kept on praying, knowing that if I forgot for a single moment that I was only a tool in God's hands, I would leave the course Jesus had set out in the hour of temptation. Then I would be no longer in the presence of the mystery of His commitment to the poorest, to those who are insignificant to the world. I would be no longer with my people, nor with those poorly clad youths climbing the steps before me, on their way to an encounter which would mark their lives.

At Castel Gondolfo, I relived the dangers of the Temptation. And because we adults had refused with one accord to play the leaders, to be anything but tools and humble witnesses of the honour paid the Fourth World, never was there a stronger and more limpid tie between us and these young people. Eighty young men and women were in a position to verify that, at the Vatican, in the midst of those who hold high rank in the Church, we sought nothing for ourselves and were concerned only with their dignity and joy. Never was there a more shining unity among them, Christians and non-Christians of all ethnic backgrounds, gathering at mass to sing and be happy together. With these young people we could from then on discuss, with no risk of being misunderstood, the service and the love they in turn owed their families, their slums, their companions.

Will we or won't we make it our common priority to stand united around the least able, who forever jeopardise whatever small degree of security our combat has achieved? This question seems to have become possible and even inevitable after Christ's Temptation in the desert. I believe it will be at the core of the dialogue between Jesus and the crowds with whom He is now going to mingle. As for me, I bear witness that even the smallest failure with regard to this question costs me my intimacy with the Lord and my joy of knowing myself to be in His footsteps. Likewise, even the smallest neglect of Christ's answers to the tempter costs me my intimacy with the most deprived families.

It is, no doubt, for this reason that I attach such importance to this event directly preceding Jesus' entering public life. We do not yet gauge all the consequences, but I feel it predicts all that the Church will be in the world without being of the world, all that Christians and religious people will have to be. Christ's life henceforth will but explain, illustrate and deepen the commitment made then for all time.

CHAPTER TWO

The Crowd, Always First to Bear Witness

Jesus has confirmed His commitment to God and to humanity. The life His Father had planned for Him from now on belongs to the people. Where will He turn His steps, to whom will He bring the Good News?

When Jesus heard that John had been put in prison,
He went away to Galilee.
He did not stay in Nazareth,
but went to live in Capernaum,
a town by Lake Galilee,
in the territory of Zebulon and Naphtali.
This was done
to make what the prophet Isaiah had said come true:

". . . Galilee, land of the Gentiles!
The people who live in darkness
will see a great light.
On those who live in the dark land of death,
the light will shine."

(Matthew 4, 12-16)

"Galilee, land of the Gentiles," says Isaiah, and commentators on the New Testament note that Matthew's emphasis here is on the ministry of Jesus choosing to reach all nations. His part of the world represents, as it were, a border territory, perpetually threatened by pagan invasions. Foreign communities have settled within. Through them, Christ will address all peoples. This is no doubt what happened. Yet the commentary seems incomplete.

For was this "Galilee of the Gentiles" a land of open boundaries and manifold encounters? Did the Galileans, poor and despised by the other Jews, nevertheless represent a cultural crossroads? In our longing to follow where Jesus walked and to feel close around us all these people chosen to receive His teachings first, let us contemplate them and try to get to know them. Through them, we shall better understand how Jesus carries through the commitment made in the desert. This is important. The most crucial guidelines for the Church, for Christians and for all people till the end of time are at stake here. Moreover, the very poorest of our own time ask to meet, know and be enabled to live in communion with these people who took precedence in Christ's life. How then must we visualise them?

I look toward areas of extreme poverty in Europe,

Africa, Latin America. Here, I see a poverty-stricken housing settlement on the outskirts of Marseilles, a dilapidated neighbourhood of the Hague, slated for a renovation that never seems to come to an end. There, I see a very poor village, surrounded by even poorer hamlets, somewhere in Latin America. I also see a bush area bordering two countries south of the Sahara, where the river is going dry and the soil is cracked, turning to dust. And in all these places I see blends of ethnic groups, people and families coming and going, people who share neither culture nor language. In Marseilles and the Hague, as in all poor areas in western Europe, native citizens, the poorest among immigrants and migrant workers, the most deprived among travellers, are all huddled together at the bottom of the social scale. They mingle with foreigners who have entered the country by fraud and others prohibited from living there. The Latin American village I have in mind is inhabited by people called "latinos," who are poor, but hold the best land and whatever modest positions of influence the community offers. In the surrounding hamlets live the descendants of a Native American Indian people, so deeply impoverished that they have nothing left to show for their cultural heritage, no outward sign, no traditional dress, at best a dialect for daily use but unfit to express complex human thoughts and feeling. As for the area south of the Sahara, where the desert claims the land, only the most deprived and exhausted cling to their arid soil. Refugees from hunger or war, soldiers, deserters from over the border pass through the hamlets as do the traders, always to be found near the very poor, exploiting their ignorance and deprivation.

The families in extreme poverty in our western cities, the landless in remote regions of developing countries, the impoverished ethnic minorities throughout the world—they all seem to share the same condition. They are most often mingled, thrust together regardless of nationality and all equally deprived of the means to live and maintain their respective cultures. They invite us to reflect on ancient Galilee. Having chosen the most vulnerable, will Jesus set out to proclaim the Good News at a crossroads where the Gentiles are represented in all their cultural wealth? Or will He rather favour a land where the culturally deprived converge, the uprooted who seemingly have little chance of serving as agents by virtue of their belonging to a nation? Would not Christ have naturally chosen the latter, knowing that those who are beyond certain limits of poverty, rejection and cultural deprivation can grasp His message immediately and be agents of the great news by virtue of their very misery? Personally, I cannot imagine Jesus choosing otherwise.

Galilee, land of the Gentiles, to be sure, since then as now the poor were often on the road, crossing borders if necessary, in search of a less harsh existence. But then, Galilee of the poor among the Gentiles mingled with the poorest among the Jews. "The people which was in darkness" included a majority of circumcised Jews who could not be said to be in darkness, as were the pagans because they did not know God. Rather, they were in darkness because the Pharisees and the doctors of law prevented the poor from obtaining true knowledge about the law of God. We are not surprised to find these people, considered impure and sinful, "in the dark land of death," confined to a border territory where blood was likely to be spilled in the course of foreign invasions. We are faced with one of these lands where conflicts between nations are acted out at the expense of the poor. This region is also a breeding ground for insurrections against the mighty, because the land is taken from the local communities and small farmers, to be consolidated in ever-larger estates. Small owners are obliged to give up their last acres, lacking the means to pay taxes and debts.

If affluent people still remained in this impoverished Galilee, was it not in part because of the abounding number of very poor? These were easy to take advantage of, defenceless in the face of those who possessed religious knowledge and power, the big landowners and the shrewd merchants. Those who exploit the very poor are not necessarily the most wealthy. They are often contractors, tradesmen, despised by the rich, but used by them as intermediaries. Unless they are poor themselves, they are often seemingly well-to-do because they manage to take advantage. of those still poorer than themselves. Anyway, a situation of such social imbalance can only worsen, as expropriation and changing relationships with the land start undermining relations among people, families and communities. The numbers of seasonal, occasional or even chronically unemployed workers increased inordinately. New, often uncertain or debasing labour relations took the place of the former terms of mutual esteem and security. These developments were also bound to influence relations with foreign communities.

In short, the Galilee where Jesus went to and fro was the land of a dislocated people, burdened with unbearable tithes, coupled with new, iniquitous taxes, its social order gradually dismantled. I feel He chose it as His land of predilection for this specific reason. All protagonists, all witnesses were in their right places there, around the essential issue of liberating humanity from excruciating poverty and total oppression against which there was no appeal. At stake here was the only liberation which would allow the world to imagine the fullness of God's love. In Galilee, Christ would not simply free the weakest but *be Himself their liberation.*

Let us now follow Jesus, henceforth in the hands of the crowd. Matthew, always concise and sparing of words, seems never to miss an occasion to confront us with this Jesus, captive of the lowly. "Large crowds followed Him from Galilee and the Ten Towns, from Jerusalem, Judea, and the land on the other side of the Jordan. . . ." "Jesus saw the crowds and went up a hill. . . ." "When Jesus came down from the hill, large crowds followed Him." "As He saw the crowds, His heart was filled with pity for them. . . ." "The crowd that gathered round Him was so large. . . ." ". . . The people heard about it, so they left their towns and followed Him by land." ". . . the people recognised Jesus. So they sent for the sick people in all the surrounding country and brought them to Jesus." "Large crowds came to Him, bringing with them the lame, the blind, the crippled, the dumb and many other sick people. . . ." "Large crowds followed Him and he healed them there." "When Jesus finished saying these things, the crowd was amazed at the way He taught." "A large crowd of people spread their cloaks on the road. . . ." "'This is the prophet Jesus, from Nazareth in Galilee,' the crowds answered." (Matthew 4-25; 5-1; 8-1; 9-36; 13-2; 14-13; 14-35; 15-30; 19-2; 7-28; 21-8 and 21-11)

The first Gospel leaves no room for doubt; the crowds and the poorest among them were the Lord's first associates. Matthew so repeatedly makes us meet Jesus, jostled and harassed by the crowds, that we feel we hear their din, the voices crying out around Him. We see the men and women pressing forward, pushing their way, and even brushing aside the disciples to come closer to the Lord and touch Him. They are entire families, fathers and mothers with children in tow, hastening along the road, families in great numbers, sometimes coming from afar, sometimes assembling in a great hurry. When Jesus occasionally wants to withdraw, He must make a special effort, or even drag Himself away. No doubt, in order to breathe a little, in order to pray, He must literally flee, as I often did myself when I was overwhelmed and had but one desire: to see these men and women no more. His patience must have no limits. He goes into the towns to teach at the synagogues, addressing the Pharisees. The Sadducees draw Him aside for questioning. He visits a private home. But always and ever, the crowd is there, pushing its way inside or waiting on the doorstep, listening, wondering, marvelling, talking and gossiping! Jesus addresses the Sadducees and "the crowd was amazed at the way He taught." Jesus takes a meal with His disciples in His own home and here come "many tax collectors and sinners" sitting down with them unceremoniously. Things happened as if the Lord, wherever He was, whatever He did and whoever His audience happened to be, was always mainly concerned with this crowd which brought Him its wretchedness, laying down at His feet the burden of its crippled and blind. As if this noisy and disorderly mob, always pressing to be in the front row, were really first and foremost in His thoughts, His heart, His tenderness, His entire design for salvation. All His patience, all His teaching were for them in the first place. Also for the others, for all humanity, but never without the crowd and its poorest.

The commentators on the Gospel tend to emphasise the variety of Christ's audiences. They note the friends and foes, the wealthy and the humble, the scholars and the ignorant, the Jews and the Gentiles. Yet, when following Jesus, we find that, while audiences vary, the crowd and the disciples are permanently present. In fact, the crowd will have to be dispersed for a moment by the high priests during Christ's arrest. ". . . They made plans to arrest Jesus secretly and put Him to death. 'We must not do it during the festival,' they said, 'or the people will riot'." (Matthew 26, 4-5)

The crowd is the Lord's native land, the place where He belongs. According to the Gospel, Jesus addresses even His own disciples through the crowd before gathering them around Him in private to tell them their mission. Why does the crowd serve Him as a first illustration and as a first channel of communication, even with His hand-picked companions? I think the crowd's presence helped the disciples understand the mission they were about to receive, which will not fail to puzzle exegetes.

> *Do not go to any Gentile territory*
> *or any Samaritan towns.*
> *Instead you are to go to those lost sheep,*
> *the people of Israel. Go and preach,*
> *"The Kingdom of Heaven is near!"*
> *Heal the sick,*
> *bring the dead back to life,*
> *heal the lepers,*
> *drive out demons.*
> *You have received without paying,*
> *so give without being paid.*

(Matthew 10, 5-8)

Why did Jesus, Himself a teacher of "Galilee of the Gentiles," urge the apostles not to go to foreign cities? Some commentators wonder. Was there a difference between what the Master did and what the disciples must do? I don't think so. The main point—as Jesus said—was to seek out the lost sheep: those lost by the house of Israel, so as to reach *all* Jews; those lost in Samaria in order to reach *all* Samaritans. My understanding of this grew slowly, thanks to the very poor who helped me get closer to Jesus amid the crowd of His day.

My memories take me back to a frigid morning in 1960 at the Camp for the Homeless in Noisy-le-Grand. Many people think that this camp began as they knew it later, in the late 1960s, a mass of totally deprived and forsaken families, misery at its peak. This was not yet the case in 1960, when families suffering different degrees of poverty were sheltered by the igloo-shaped huts lining the unpaved roads which turned sodden in wintertime. Some were French working-class families with incomes too low to cover a normal minimum rent; others were temporarily uprooted and without a proper roof, after being repatriated from the former colonies. There were also households of unemployed migrant workers and of travelling people, seeking to settle down. Finally, there were families in hard-core poverty, burdened from one generation to the next with underemployment, ignorance and disease, with lack of housing and income, since the beginning of this century or even earlier. On the morning I recall, all were outside, the utterly deprived as well as the most organised, all gathered around a representative of the district's government. The night watchman just returned from work stood next to his unemployed neighbour whose only living was in his cart filled with early-morning salvaged scraps. With them was another unemployed head of a family who lacked even the strength to rummage through the garbage cans or to salvage rags from the city dump, and who spent whole days prostrate on his mattress on the bare floor of his hut. The women were also there, and the children who in spite of their age did not attend school. Grandma Lassagne had brought her two mentally handicapped grandchildren, whom she normally hid from the social workers. The blind violinist groped his way to follow them all. On this

51

frosty winter morning, they were all out in the open together, loudly bemoaning their poverty and their misfortune to be living in so damnable a place.

And I, their priest, was there, trying as they did to reason with the official, trying also to protect him from those who shoved and threatened him. And as I watched them all, these words of the Gospel came to me as a shock: "As He saw the crowds, His heart was filled with pity for them, because they were worried and helpless, like sheep without a shepherd." (Matthew 9, 36)

I used to see this same crowd in greater or smaller numbers when we walked the Stations of the Cross on Good Friday, as we continued to do because the families always attended. I also welcomed them at Sunday mass and, in greater numbers, on Christmas Eve and Easter. And I had seen this crowd become poorer and poorer as the years went by and the better-off families were gradually resettled outside this hell. The people could no longer hide their rising numbers of crippled, of bodies distorted by rheumatism, scoliosis or rickets, of trembling limbs, of mouths with permanently rotting teeth. More and more men, women and children in these conditions came up to me at every corner. I could not avoid them, for they would go out of their way to cross my path during the day, or knock on my door at night. "Father, come quickly, my child is dying." "Father, I have no money left to buy the children milk." And over the years, as the Fourth World Movement grew, I met this crowd over and over in countless other districts throughout France: "La Cerisaie" and "Le Moulin Neuf" in Stains, "Les Emouleuses" in Créteil,

"La Campa" in La Courneuve, "Les Francs Moisins" in Saint Denis. . . . Throughout France, and gradually all over Europe, this very same crowd materialised before my eyes.

In all these areas of extreme poverty and ill-repute, the prophecy "He will be called a Nazarene" returned to my mind unrelentingly, as did the slur always tagged onto this indication of Christ's origins, "What good can come from Nazareth?" Was I not a witness of the same contempt always inflicted upon the very poor, at all times, in all places? "If I give my right address, the boss will kick me out, and fast." "Our kids have to sit in the back of the class, just because of where we live." One Christmas Day, a mother explained her panic to me: "My baby was born last night, but he was dead. I don't dare go and tell the registrar. If they know we live in this shantytown, they'll say we killed him! Then what will become of us?" Jesus, the crowds of Galilean families, the poverty-stricken families in the most deprived housing areas in our industrialised countries. . . , where did the Gospel begin, where did it end? To me they are all one.

Crowds of people too miserable to behave unobtrusively, crowds always ready to emerge because they have nothing important to give a routine to their day. . . . Those who have even a little, regular workers, tradespeople, cannot gather this way, unawares, seeking the unexpected, seizing any opportunity. I had never seen those people leaving their homes on a moment's notice in my former parishes: "Mrs. Fontaine tells me this is Palm Sunday, I must hurry to the chapel. . . ." "The Fourth World volunteers are coming for a meeting at the kindergarten. I'm going there right away. . . ." Those who have a field to till, a time clock to punch, a shop to tend, lead an orderly life. They attend to their business and eventually to the affairs of God, all in due time, duly planned in advance. The priest and the Levite in the parable of the Good Samaritan had no time to linger with the wounded man at the roadside. Hasn't this always been the case?

Most important, no doubt, those who are more or less able to organise and master their existence need not rush off after a messenger at first notice. They are not tormented and anxious to the point of constantly being on the lookout for news, for help, and—why not?—for a saviour. Who but the humble, the poor, the rejected are always waiting for the man who will bring about change, the guide, the master? Exegetes have said much about the motives of various groups of the Jewish population for flocking around Christ. They note the political currents in search of a leader who would free Israel and found a new society as prophesied. Are we sufficiently aware that the very poor must have participated in such movements in their very own way? They certainly did not possess the political consciousness of the better off, but they must have shared the deeply rooted expectation of a saviour. Personally, I have never met groups in extreme poverty, be they in France or Haïti, in the Netherlands or Central Africa, in Guatemala or Thailand, who would not share this sort of constant waiting for a saviour who would not merely change immediate living conditions, but would transform the entire human existence.

In fact, as soon as I began my ministry among a totally deprived French population, I felt that living among these families meant residing among the crowd surrounding Jesus. These homeless people, what else could they be but the mass of very poor whom Christ Himself saw as "worried and helpless, like sheep without a shepherd"? These words still come to my mind, as they did recently while travelling through some hamlets way out in the African bush. We had decided to set up a Fourth World volunteer team there, at the very end of an almost impassable track. As we sat under a tree or a straw roof to converse with the villagers, they asked, "Will you stay with us?" "We shall not remain here now," we said, "this is just a first visit to find out if you would agree. If you do, we shall be back." "But then why don't you stay right away?" Of course, there were no big crowds in this forlorn and dried out region. But there was still the same feeling of urgency, despite the heat and the fever. There was still the same hope for the unexpected. Women laid their hands on the arms of Ruth, the volunteer who would return. "Stay with us, tomorrow is Christmas." What did they expect from this young white woman who had not yet learned their language, and did not even carry a stock of anti-malaria drugs?

Today's poor are continually bringing us back to the very heart of the Gospel, close to Jesus whose eyes never left the crowd of the humble. That crowd seems to me so similar to those I see today. It hastens to and fro in the Gospel, leaving the villages in a rush, with no thought for tomorrow. It walks for hours, as do those villagers in Central Africa today, covering miles and miles before dawn to attend mass. It reacts spontaneously, wonders and marvels, and yet never tries to implicate Jesus in a mere discussion of ideas. What exquisite tenderness the Lord shows these people, what sensitivity to who they really are, to what they hope for and to what they can understand! Between Jesus and the crowds reigns such profound harmony that no sooner are they dispersed than they gather again, wherever He appears. They follow Him, venturing even to prophesy, "Hosannah to the Son of David," thus rousing indignation among the high priests.

But can we surmise such profound harmony, knowing that the hour will come when the crowd will forsake Him? We are told that the people betrayed their saviour. "The Jewish people refuse to believe in Him." The families in deep poverty today, however, teach us a finer perception, leading to a quite different meditation. They tell us how difficult it is to develop logical thinking, consistent opinions and firm attitudes when one is deprived of culture and even of elementary schooling. For centuries, it has been said that crowds are as credulous as children, that they are inconsistent, shallow and easily diverted. Give them bread and games and they will fall in line. This is an insult to the poor, whose real misfortune is being deprived of education and of correct, factual information. Those who hoard knowledge keep these means to themselves. In 1983, some eight million citizens in the member states of the European Community were estimated to be both poor and illiterate. There is little chance that these numbers have decreased. Given these conditions, the ignorant make the best possible use of their daily experience, their memory, their feeling for things and for people. If only they were given more freedom to live and act as they think best in their poverty areas, they would eventually fine-tune their logic and systematise their memories. Then they could assert themselves as what they are, and as Jesus saw them, namely as experts on extreme poverty and as authorities on human nature. Then they would truly be the spokesmen of Christ, who has chosen to be one of them, one with them.

Fourth World families, however, are impeded in our present-day towns and villages as the poor were shackled by the scribes and Pharisees in the House of Israel. There is always an agency, there are always people to tell them they are fools who do everything wrong and should not live the way they do: "You had better put your child in a foster home, it would cost you much less." "Why do you insist on staying with your husband when he is out of work and has taken to drinking? I could help you register as a one-parent family." The frightened mother can think of no reply. Late at night she will come to me, "Father, my husband and I, we loved each other. He is the father of my children, he has been good to me. Am I to leave him now that things have gone wrong and he is unhappy?" But she and I know that unless she musters an undreamt of wealth of steadfastness and ingenuity, she will be compelled to conform to someone else's logic. I have seen so many families who, despite incomparable staying power, had to yield in the end to the arguments of the educated. I, therefore, cannot accept the judgments passed on the crowds that supposedly forsook Jesus.

Christ Himself, in any case, never said that the crowds "refused to believe." He differentiated between those who refused—the Pharisees, the doctors of law, the scribes—and those prevented from believing by these authority figures—the poor and especially the most vulnerable. The latter, because of their very helplessness, have a greater need to believe in something, to pin their hopes on someone. Those who ignore this will never understand their bursts of enthusiasm, their impetuous infatuations with strong and commanding personalities. They cannot accept the crowd's obstinate expectation of a miracle. But Jesus, who knew His own so well, never forgot that they longed to believe in Him.

He was well aware that the impassioned crowds were saying, "Isn't He the Son of David?" He never smoothed their path to God by brushing aside the true demands of faith. But He never failed to distinguish clearly between the guardians of doctrine and law and the credulous crowd, easily impressed and readily submissive because of its very ignorance. His condemnation of those who prevent the lowly from believing is terrifying.

How terrible for you,
teachers of the Law and Pharisees!
You hypocrites! You lock the door to the Kingdom
of Heaven
in people's faces,
and you yourselves don't go in,
nor do you allow in those who are trying to enter!

(Matthew 23, 13)

How terrible for you teachers of the Law!
You have kept the key
that opens the door to the house of knowledge;
you yourselves will not go in and you stop those
who are trying to go in!

(Luke 11, 52)

How in fact did the Pharisees and doctors of law manage to shut out the people of good will? The Pharisees and scribes, the experts in law, did so by not practising mercy, by crushing the people with burdens that they themselves "would not move with one of their fingers." This indication is important, for it also explains who were prevented from approaching God, from believing in Jesus, namely, those overwhelmed with burdens which the well-to-do could refuse, those who needed to see mercy granted to them to believe in it, yet who were constantly denied it.

Jesus knows that the humble are no more righteous or just than the powerful, that they are not necessarily either merciful or loving toward the weakest among them. He did not join the world of the wretched because it was a world of virtue, but because it was and still is a world of suffering and helplessness in the face of misfortune. Jesus joined it because here converge all life's vicissitudes and all society's mistakes, all injustices, exploitation and oppression, and also—this is important—all abuse of the goodwill of the ignorant. This is why in all humility we may feel close to Jesus when we renounce our privileges ourselves, setting out to find the lost sheep in areas of extreme poverty. He knew all that we ourselves experience from day to day: the monopolising of the scarce means available, the mutual distrust and hostility and, above all, the constant temptation of the poor to brutalise or to desert the most wretched among them, in order to somehow make good themselves. But Jesus also knew why the poor are undependable, why they can so easily be abused. He knew why they lack the arguments needed to defend a conviction in the face of the learned.

Jesus realises that the very poorest, whatever they believe in their heart of hearts, will be at the mercy of those who by virtue of their intellectual and social superiority will force them to cry, "Barrabas!" Not only do the Pharisees, scribes and doctors of law thus intimidate the crowd. The small farmers, the merchants, the artisans, all those among the Jewish people who have developed political awareness and expect Jesus to free the land from the Romans, will do likewise. They are deeply disappointed not to have found in Him the leader who would put an end to the Roman occupation and restore prosperity. They too will be easily instigated to demand His execution and, in turn, they will urge the very poor to deny him. They are closer to them than are the Pharisees and their attitude will serve as a model: "If they disown Jesus, they must have good reason. . . ."

I myself have often witnessed how difficult it is for the most deprived to defend what they want to believe. Particularly so at the Camp in Noisy-le-Grand where public authorities kept on telling the families that they would fare much better if I left. At night, when these officials were no longer around, we would be left there face to face: the families, the first Fourth World volunteers and myself. Then people would come and knock on my door, as ashamed as was Nicodemus. The very men who had circulated a petition requesting my departure would say, "Father, you're not really going to leave us?" "Father, if they take away your shack, we'll all leave this place with you. We'll build you a real cabin, you'll see!" Would not Jesus have understood infinitely better than I this distress of the poor, never knowing on what or on whom to rely?

> *Jerusalem, Jerusalem!*
> *You kill the prophets*
> *and stone the messengers God has sent you!*
> *How many times I have wanted*
> *to put my arms round all your people,*
> *just as a hen gathers her chicks under her wings,*
> *but you would not let me!*
> (Matthew 23, 37)

In the eyes of Jesus, who actually stoned God's envoys? What did He mean by gathering them together and what dissension was this meant to heal? If the people had been united, mercy established and burdens shared, would the crowd have been led to forsake the Lord? Would Jesus have been rejected by His own? When I look at Fourth World families and also at some less rejected ones in our own time, I find it unbearable that the profound and enduring alliance between Jesus and the crowds could be denied. The crowds of the humble were not so much inconsistent as vulnerable, even in their search for God. Closing the door on our contemplation of the true identity of this crowd and on its plight means an incalculable loss. Did Jesus not love these people precisely for their vulnerability? In misrepresenting these families who had so little control over their own ideas, we lose an opportunity to fathom our responsibility and acquire more humility in the presence of such misery. Jesus' whole life was a refusal not only of their material poverty, but of their intellectual and spiritual deprivation. Christ unrelentingly defended the intelligence and the faith of the lowly.

His alliance with them was all the more profound for its clairvoyance. Jesus Christ never mistook extreme sensitivity to injustice for the ability to practise justice oneself. When poverty becomes excessive, it rarely leaves much room for being just, loving and merciful. The very poor are aware of this. They are desperately seeking redemption and salvation. Christ therefore never exalts the poor's righteousness. They will be the first to hear that they must be converted to the God of love and *forgiveness*.

How often have I heard people assert before a town official, a trade union delegate, a police inspector, or a Caritas officer, "My neighbour is a lazy bum. I have nothing to do with him. I'm not like the people around here, they're all gangsters." It is a way to defend one's reputation in an area where deprivation breeds theft and violence. Yet the man who so betrays his neighbour one day may well lend him his bicycle or take his children in for a meal the next. He knows that, "gangsters" or not, the family has no money left to buy food. Is there reason to believe that the very poor of Galilee and Judea were in a position to refrain from such betrayals? They were probably no less torn between the dire necessity of getting by themselves at the cost of their neighbours, and the profound need to live in peace with all. When poverty, helplessness and insecurity are beyond bounds, they wear out what is best in people. Their efforts to resist such inner destruction are all the more admirable. I have often marvelled at people's capacity, in an utterly poor housing area, to continue showing proof of friendship, solidarity or love. In fact, it takes an attentive eye and delicate feeling to recognise such proof. People's gestures and acts often appear so unpretentious and clumsy, so insignificant and negligible when one does not consider the obstacles which must be overcome.

The main point of course is not to appraise these ever-renewed efforts at their true value. We are not to take the place of God. The main point is that we act as witnesses, in a position to say, "I see you as responsible for your own deeds, you are free to choose and here you have made a choice that will benefit a fellow human being." Indeed, the mysterious intimacy between Jesus and the crowd seems to constantly express itself in one fundamental agreement. For Jesus and the crowd seem to agree on what people are responsible for and what enhances their dignity, on the one hand, and what they cannot control and where God must come in to understand, forgive, heal and save them, on the other. We never hear a false note in this continuing dialogue going on over the heads of all the other people who may be on the scene. "Here is what God gives and here is what you, the humble, owe Him as His free and responsible children." In this dialogue, the most wretched are going to hold a central place.

For in the midst of the crowd, or in its wake, we are now going to discover human beings more overwhelmed, more wretched and rejected than most. It is they who are going to make us truly understand Jesus' warning to the "large crowd" that listened "with delight":

> *Watch out for the teachers of the Law,*
> *who like to walk around in their long robes*
> *and be greeted with respect in the marketplace,*
> *who choose the reserved seats in the synagogues*
> *and the best places at feasts.*
> *They take advantage of widows*
> *and rob them of their homes,*
> *and then make a show of saying long prayers.*

(Mark 12, 38-40)

Watch out, do not imitate them, says Jesus. You too are tempted, and following their example will bring upon you, as upon them, "the most severe punishment." Your teachers may misguide you, but that does not make you righteous by comparison nor exempt you from watching out for your own errors.

Concern for the poorest and for their place within the community will be at the very heart of all that will now pass and be said between Jesus and the crowds flocking around Him in their anguish, amazement or all-consuming hope. Crowds largely made up of poor people, and where the dividing line between the poor and the wretched was wavering, the lepers never far from the healthy, the prostitutes not far from respected women. Let us behold Jesus among them. Nevermore till the end of time will He cease offering their hope to the Father.

CHAPTER THREE

"...the Lame, the Blind, the Crippled, the Mute, and Many Others..."

All Christians do not see with the same eyes these men and women crowding the roads, hurrying along the riverbanks with their children, not knowing where they are going nor how long they will be away. To pray, to live, and to be active amid the Fourth World is to tread a privileged path toward Christ, where He comes and goes among His chosen companions. How can we love Him without loving those He placed first in His life and teaching? And how can we love them if we cannot make out their faces? The Fourth World families have shown me a way, revealing the signposts and distinctive marks which would help me meet and recognise them. But many people today allow themselves to be led by others who in fact live in a very different sort of world. They do not always seem to reach the same Christ who renounced all political power. Neither do they seem to meet the same harassed and helpless crowds, nor to discover the excluded squatting in the sunken roads outside town. But these differences should not entice us into circuitous debates. I am convinced that we all seek Christ's face in those we consider most downtrodden and abandoned. The most important thing is that we search for Christ together, never stopping at an already familiar group of people who may block our view of another even poorer one. Even in Jesus' time, the crowds often hid their lepers, their cripples and insane, who were more prostrate than most, on the outskirts of their villages, way out in the countryside or in caves up in the hills.

All through the ages, the Church has resumed this search taught by Christ. It has borne witness to the mystery of the common fate of the poor of our own time and of the crowds on whom the Lord had mercy, of the poorest among them, whom He healed. Throughout its history, the Church has taken to heart the warning, "And the poor shall be with you forever." Its weakness is its faltering memory, its forgetting the faces, the lives, the universal signs of extreme poverty. This shortness of memory gives rise to unnecessary misapprehensions: "The poor of the days of Jesus are in no way comparable to those we meet nowadays in the cities of Western Europe or Latin America" ... "Today's poor have nothing in common with those of the Middle Ages" ... "One cannot compare poverty in Africa with that prevailing in New York or in Chicago." What do we really know about it? On the basis of what observations, what memory, what information do we support such assertions? We should in fact not have to discuss these things. We and the entire Church should be in a position to recognise the poor and the most deprived of all centuries, since they are the heirs of the crowds of Galilee and Jerusalem.

That we are unable to do this is our weakness and the weakness of the whole Church, which does not keep its memory up-to-date with respect to that part of humanity which is so essential to itself. The Church has never betrayed the poor, although it may not always have declared its fidelity clearly enough. But it is often defenceless in the face of critical minds who charge it with always being in league with the privileged. For however closely the Church may have been intertwined with the poor, its grasp of their common history remains faulty. Nor does it teach that history which is in fact its own. This perhaps explains the difficulty the Church experiences in knowing and teaching the history of the poor and excluded surrounding Christ. Yet, how can we approach Him and those around Him, if not through those whose very lives bear Him witness through the ages and even today? The Church's mission remains today what it was in the past, namely to stay firmly rooted in its perpetual search for the poorest, keeping in mind the lessons, the signs and distinctive marks learnt over two thousand years.

We can all contribute to the Church's task of putting in order the immense heritage of ordinary daily knowledge. We can do so, provided we make head-

way in the contemplation and love of Christ submerged in extreme poverty. ("Jesus was terribly
poor," John Paul II affirmed to a delegation of young
people from the Fourth World at Castel Gondolfo in
1982.) Provided also that we remain close to those
who have always embodied the deepest human misery. By living in severely poverty-stricken surround-
ings, I was bound to learn myself how the misery of
the crippled, the blind, the handicapped can be infinitely deeper there than in less deprived areas. Who
could be more helpless? Facing them, I could not but
face the question of the crippled, the paralytics, the
deaf and mute in Jesus' time. The lame, the epileptic,
and the mentally handicapped in the most underprivileged housing areas thus became my teachers
and my guides.

They forced me to look much more closely at the
handicapped in the paths of Galilee. First, they
taught me not to consider today's disabled as all
equally poor and despised. They also induced me to
have a better look at similarly afflicted people in the
poorest countries of Africa and Asia. Even among
deprived peoples, the situations of the diseased and
the crippled can vary considerably, depending on
whether or not they belong to a relatively well-
organised family, village or urban community able to
provide at least some protection. The disabled of the
most severely deprived groups seemed to me to go
through sheer hell.

The latter are to be found more often out on the
roads, holding out their bowls in the marketplace or
at the temple door. They are publicly exposed even
in ethnic groups whose custom it is to keep the

handicapped within the family precincts. The poorest among the crippled—or rather the crippled from the poorest communities—are more frequently left to fend for themselves, crawling about the marketplaces seeking alms. Sometimes their own relatives force them into this shameful exhibition because the family is too poor to feed them. Similarly, epileptics are still thrown into the fire in some parts of the world where there are no possibilities whatsoever to offer them a decent living.

Were these human realities so very different in Christ's day? When I meet the paralysed man in the Gospel who had no friends and could not get to the pool when it started swirling, I cannot help thinking of a blind man who was relegated to the camp at Noisy-le-Grand. No one could guide him any longer to the Paris subway where he used to scrape on a battered violin, earning just enough for him and his disabled mother to get by. When I meet the crowd in the Gospel, pressing in on Jesus to lay their sick and possessed at His feet, I cannot help but think that, were Jesus to pass through our cities today, the people living in emergency shelters, slums and the poorest housing settlements would be the very first to rush to Him this way. As in the past, they would surge forth in noisy confusion, heedless of time and order, following this almost crazy faith which stirs within a people kept from power and knowledge, and therefore totally devoid of scepticism.

We must imagine the trust one needs in order to lay bare one's wounds, to show a frightening disease, to display a disfigurement which shocks and repels even the most well-meaning. People do not reveal their infirmities that way in hatred or revolt. Whatever their cultural background, they never show them at all, if they can help it. The initiative of some who invite Jesus to come to their homes should not surprise us. Those were the people who enjoyed some affluence and position, as did the centurion. Only the very poor can be induced to bring forward their disabled in large numbers, their complete hopelessness giving rise all at once to most desperate action and wildest hopes. In the lands where Jesus walked, there were undoubtedly many more poor than better-off. Moreover, among the poor, the sick and the disabled were certainly more numerous than among the better-off. When we consider that the poorest, the diseased, the most rejected were undoubtedly those most easily carried away by Jesus, then how could we fail to see the Lord constantly surrounded not so much by the "good people" as by a mass of men and women in a most pitiful condition? Then we are bound to bow to the extraordinary understanding and complicity between Jesus and those most harassed among people. We must bow to this profound consensus which, again and again, culminates in these words, "You are healed, you are saved."

Indeed, the healing of the very poor who could but offer Him total trust, seems to become a continuous means of communication between Jesus and the crowds. "Go then, for your faith has healed you." "You have believed in Me and in God, therefore everything has become possible. God would never abandon those who come to Him as you do, having no recourse but Him." Could Jesus have spoken and acted this way with less helpless people? I feel the message then could not have been the same. To be sure, Jesus has healed or even raised from the dead people who were not poor. But they are exceptions and the reason for these miracles is carefully explained in each case. This gives us even more reason to believe that for the crowd and its most rejected, there was no need for explaining. The very gesture of each healing sufficiently expressed Jesus' solidarity. A most concrete solidarity: "I know your plight, for I share it; I know you want to be healed and can ask this only of God, since the world has forsaken you."

When I look at the poor today, at the very poor still among them or even by them, I realize that Jesus could have no other relationship with them than one based on mercy. How could He have done otherwise? Today, as in the past, God's mercy is made an object of rational thinking. The Pharisees had seen fit to attach a number of conditions to divine mercy. Jesus bitterly reproached them for this. Today, we have our own ways of rationalising God's infinite mercy, rendering it conditional in order to be more efficient. But did Jesus not come to earth precisely to re-establish God's efficiency? "Since you have no one but Him, God cannot forsake you."

I think of the women who would come to my office in a permanent state of exhibition of their misery, their bodies distorted by difficult pregnancies, their faces reddened by drinking. They would sit there, sometimes for hours on end, complaining about one thing and another, asking for a few pen-

72

nies. Then long periods of silence would follow before they would get down to the real question: "Father, my children have no respect for me" ... "Father, my neighbours hate me" ... "My husband has beaten me again. True, my children have no shoes; yet I do all I can but you know I am sick." I would also know that one of them no longer had a stove, a neighbour having offered a good price for it at one of those moments when a family has to choose between eating and keeping warm. Another one of these women had been left by her husband. All these mothers came to me in search of advice, of a sign of understanding. But with me they always needed time to get down to essentials. With Jesus, I said to myself, they would have been understood without even uttering a word. He would have made the one gesture needed to bring home to them that He knew and understood. The most precious moments I passed with one of these women—Madame Estampe—were when she just sat there silently, calm and beauty slowly coming over her face. Finally, she would get up and leave me: "Thank you, Father." As if all had been said and understood between us, her life having recovered its meaning.

At such moments, one feels a little closer to Jesus, brother of the poorest, who put into good order the affairs of divine mercy. I had given Madame Estampe all the money left in my pocket and which I should no doubt have spent more rationally. I had taken all my time, when efficiency would have urged me to count my hours and plan them meticulously. But in this place of woe, a mother in desperation had been offered the occasion to make me feel her pain, her expectation and her hope. Some may say that I was indeed far from "changing structures," from revolution and justice. I don't know about that. All I know is that I was at the source of the reversal of the world's establishment, since I myself had once more given up all idea of being efficient and having things under control, my deepest concern being that Fourth World families would know they were important. After all, the structures or programmes they count on first of all are those that will express human fellowship, dignity, and the respect of other people's thinking.

Mme Estampe is now dead. Her husband, who had remained with her in spite of many quarrels, became a Fourth World militant for some time. One of their daughters is now an active member of a political party. Many parents, and many of their sons and daughters whom I knew at the time, have taken similar paths. I feel they did not need me to do that. What they needed, first of all, was to be convinced that extreme poverty had in no way altered their humanity, their status as children of God. They needed most of all to be reassured that their clumsiness, their violence, the impossibility of their living in peace within the family or among neighbours were all wiped out. They needed to know they were forgiven at each new effort of reconciliation, at each desperate question, "What am I to do, that my children may be proud of me and love me?" "What can I do so that my husband will stop shouting at me?" Mme Estampe sitting silently in my office meant all that. "I can bear all this shame no longer, I simply cannot go on feeling guilty all the time in the face of my family, despicable in the eyes of the whole neighbourhood. I know I am rude to them, I know I neglect my household." She had her very own way of getting all this across to me, never omitting to make me understand somehow that she had had an honourable upbringing, having been taught to know good from evil. "I was brought up by the nuns," she would say, not so much to raise herself in the esteem of a priest as to remind me what our relationship should be.

If Madame Estampe had crossed Jesus' path, she and her children would have been part of the crowd, part of the poorest for whom the only convincing message was twofold: "God heals you, God saves you." Others might be content with being only healed or only saved. For the very poor, the two gifts were inextricably linked. One alone could be neither significant nor liberating. Jesus' words and His acts were equally indispensable to them and they were in a position to fathom all the significance of these acts. "Turn away from your sins, because the Kingdom of Heaven is near." (Matthew 4, 17) They had the ears to hear the messenger "preaching the Good News about the Kingdom, and healing people who had all kinds of disease and sickness." (Matthew 4, 23)

John the Baptist, for one, received an unequivocal reply to his question, "Are you the one who was to come?" His disciples returned, reporting, "The blind can see, the lame can walk, the lepers are made clean, the deaf hear, the dead are brought back to life, and the Good News is preached to the poor." (Matthew 11, 3-5) John, well versed in the prophecies, thus learned that a significant phase of God's overall design had commenced. A phase of a faultlessly consistent design, beginning with the birth of the Son as an excluded child, passing through the Temptation in the desert, and ending with His shameful death on the Cross. The healing and evangelisation of the poor were the surest signs that Jesus was the one who must come to achieve the Kingdom, a Kingdom in which immediate mercy and salvation over time are intimately linked. With this in mind, and looking through the eyes of the poorest, we may better understand Jesus' reply to Satan: "Man cannot live on bread alone, but needs every word that God speaks." (Matthew 4, 4) For people in total deprivation, this is evident. Fourth World families today say so all the time, "True, we have no drinking water, and living knee-deep in stink and mud exhausts us. But the worst of it is having to get on the bus, your shoes caked with mud. Then they all know where you come from and they point at you. . . ." "As for me, with my mother I never ate to my heart's content. The same goes for my kids; I often lack what it takes to feed them. Yet for them, things are different, for at least they know their mother loves them." That man does not live on bread alone, I feel, is an important reminder for the better-off, so that they may learn to share not only the bread but also human dignity. As for the poor, they need not be reminded. To them, it is an obvious reality, painfully experienced in everyday life.

What makes this reality all the harder is that families and groups who suffer most from their fruitless search for respect, love and peace also have the greatest difficulty in being respectful, loving and peaceful in their own homes and communities. As I said before, they too have to face the temptation of Jesus in the desert again and again. "My application for housing is coming through at the Town Hall. Father Joseph says I might stay on a while, keep on helping the others. . . . That's all very well, but you don't imagine I would miss this chance to leave."

The headlong flight of the least poor from areas of extreme deprivation, like the temptation to exploit their more underprivileged neighbours, is the mark of areas of poverty and famine in Latin America too. The same rift in patterns of solidarity also invades certain villages in the heart of Africa, despite its well-deserved reputation for a strong sense of family and community. Should we not have expected this?

Is it likely, indeed, that people whose self-confidence has been undermined by excessive poverty will have enough self-respect to be true to the given word and sufficient strength to uphold brotherly relations with their kin? Can we expect totally deprived families, urban areas or villages bereft of all outside help to live in peace, solidarity and self-denial? What we observe around the world goes to prove the opposite: in zones of absolute poverty, violence between inhabitants flares up at any occasion of discord. Hatred between tribes, between women of the same household is roused at the slightest motive for jealousy. The most vulnerable are at times the victims of sheer cruelty.

When meditating on these observations, I return with even more bliss to the Gospel. Christ makes the life experiences of the humble and the rejected so totally His own. As soon as He enters public life, He offers answers so painfully awaited. Jesus often expresses Himself through parables, images and analogies. This in itself means that He spoke to the very poor. Of course, He also addressed the affluent, teaching them and often confounding them, invalidating their logic. But, above all, He knew that the very poor are not given the means to develop abstract thinking. He knew they needed illustrations taken from their daily existence. More important, His parables, intended to be understood by the poorest, contain lessons and guidelines of utmost relevance to them. Jesus never merely tells them He shares their pains. Nor does He simply heighten their awareness of the injustice they suffer. He speaks to them first of their responsibilities, of what they owe to God and their fellow men and women.

The Beatitudes should not induce us to take an angelical view of the poor and the humble. The law remains the same for all: "Do not think that I have come to do away with the Law of Moses and the teachings of the prophets. I have come, not to do away with them, but to make their teachings come true." (Matthew 5, 17) And all that Matthew called the "teachings," following the Beatitudes, goes equally for the very poor, the disciples, and all the people gathered there. Reconciliation, renouncing lust, fidelity to one's spouse, keeping one's word, loving one's enemies, giving alms, praying and fasting without ostentation... could we think for a single moment that the poor did not feel an acute need for encouragement on all these points? Could we imagine that Jesus would not address them first, knowing in His infinite tenderness how much they needed to be comforted, rehabilitated and given responsibility? To be given responsibility, not in the manner of the Pharisees who judged by traditional behaviour and rites, but responsibility before God and one's neighbours for one's purity of heart and the efforts within one's reach. Christ never treats the poor as if they are just. Nor does He insult them by treating them as totally irresponsible victims, with no role to play in the advent of the Kingdom of justice, love and truth that He has proclaimed. On the contrary, He declares them children of God, and therefore endowed like all God's children with freedom of choice, however narrow: the freedom to forgive, to love, to be faithful, to deprive themselves for the benefit of others. Jesus does what the world never seems capable of doing: He trusts the poorest. They are going to free themselves. All He holds forth is this extraordinary promise, without which His exhortation might have seemed almost a mockery: "Ask, and you will receive; seek, and you will find; knock, and the door will be opened to you." (Matthew 7, 7) In other words, "I know it will be difficult for you, but do not fear. God is with you."

All through my life, I have been able to measure how essential this promise is to the poorest. For what does it really mean to ask people to forgive one another when they live in overcrowded housing, the stairways littered with rubbish, everyone forced to endure misfortunes, desolation and private quarrels under the scrutiny of the entire community? The neighbours' dogs defile one's doorstep and their children steal the few painfully salvaged belongings one has stocked in the cellar. Can we imagine what it sometimes costs people not to hate the very existence of those neighbours whose children have caused the police to come in for a round-up, or who have involved one's own children in a brawl? Even the faces marked by malnutrition, the voices turned shrill from having to make themselves heard in the unending noise are not only detestable, but virtually unbearable. When one is perpetually made to feel like an inferior being, an object of ridicule because of one's ignorance and clumsiness, when one is always badly dressed and housed in shameful conditions, one is bound to blame and take revenge on the neighbourhood. "It's because of them that my boss does not respect me." "It's because of them that the police are here all the time."

No one needs to live in mutual understanding more than these families. They constantly have to ask for some kind of help from those close by, when they have so many reasons to feel bitter toward them. "They broke the stairwell light bulbs again. I can't see a thing when I take my kids downstairs." "The neighbours have dumped their rubbish on my doorstep again. So I'm the one who gets yelled at for not sweeping the landing." Merely for day-to-day survival in a minimum of harmony, one should be able to forgive and forget. But then, how can one avoid being overwhelmed by bitterness, when the real or imagined wrongs of the neighbourhood wound one so deeply? In the Fourth World, we may meet a family we had lost sight of for years and hear its members ever repeating the same recriminations against a parent who caused them to lose their job or failed to return a loan. A 45-year-old man may tell us as if it happened yesterday, "My father was a violent man, he brutalised my mother. It's because of him that she fell ill. To me, he said I'd better clear out." He may have told us this twenty times or more. Ten years later, he will start bewailing his boyhood with the very same words all over again. Emaciated, afflicted by a dislocated hip from having carried burdens too heavy too young, tense and talking too loud, he does not easily attract friends. No doubt he needs more than others to know he had parents who loved him. His resentment is all the more inordinate.

Such never-ending grudges are of course not particular to the most deprived. They exist in almost every village. They are, however, more frequent where families are extremely dependent on one another, cut off from outside recourse and diversion. I have known such enmities between families, passed on from one generation to another, in my rural parishes. Their spite was all the more irrepressible, as their community was more isolated and they had to watch over their possessions that much more carefully to avoid falling into poverty. As for the poorest among these families, the often age-old reproof on the part of the village weighed on their existence to the point of rendering impossible any friendship between their children and the other youngsters of the community.

These very basic human realities, I feel, are universal. I meet them again and again on all continents. Therefore, when contemplating Jesus in the crowd, I marvel at all these things which link humanity throughout time, space and cultures. I listen to the words the Lord addresses to the poor of His day, drawn from their very existence, and I think that all I have to do is to repeat them to the poor today. I know of no words that would be better suited to the ears, hearts and minds of the very poorest of our own time. "Nobody has ever talked like this man!" said the guardians of the temple sent out to arrest Him. (John 7, 46) "If this is how Jesus spoke, then I believe in Him," said Mr. Paquignon, father of six children living in a garden shack on the outskirts of Bessancourt.

We need not be surprised when Matthew notes, "When Jesus finished saying these things, the crowd was amazed at the way He taught. He wasn't like the teachers of the Law; instead, he taught with authority." (Matthew 7, 28-9) Exegetes say that what is meant here is Jesus' authority as Son of God. Yet when the crowds credit the Lord with authority, I feel it must also be because they recognise in Him the envoy of God who speaks in full knowledge of human existence. We should remember that the poor throughout the world credit with authority first and foremost those who know the realities of life, especially of *their* lives. "Here is a man who knows life, who understands what it's all about," is a remark expressing true respect on the part of people who rather tend to shrug their shoulders when listening to the learned, the intellectuals, the scribes of their time. "They will never understand" is what they say after most speeches.

It seems clear to me that the crowds saw Jesus as the man who understood all. He proved it by healing the diseases and afflictions of the very poor who crossed his path. There was no need for Him to explain. His was the first and essential act of God in respect of people whose suffering was beyond all bearing. Such a gesture was meant not to alleviate but to destroy extreme poverty while saving its victims, because being blind, being an invalid or a leper in misery means being deprived of the means to undertake even the slightest effort to show oneself to be a child of God. Having to suffer disease when in dire poverty means being dehumanised. The sick can have no thought, make no gesture of human fellowship. Neither can they rouse these gestures on the part of their kin. In situations of excessive poverty, one's infirmity becomes insufferable for those around one. We might well forget this in our welfare societies, in our modern hospitals. But he who lives in a poverty area in Dublin, in broken-down housing in Glasgow or in a desolate housing project outside Barcelona cannot forget. People in drought-ridden regions of Central Africa or Chad cannot forget. Poverty-stricken bodies are sometimes difficult to look at. Imagine them moreover crippled, blind, deaf, leprous. . . .

I feel that Christ attended to His Father's affairs when healing those bodies. Among the very poor, He could not have done otherwise. There was no other choice. Either we let ourselves be repulsed by fellow human beings altered beyond recognition, or we embrace them. Between stoning the leper who comes near the village and going out to him with open arms, there is no middle ground. The attitude of Fourth World volunteers around me seems to confirm this. They have chosen to dedicate their lives to the service of the poorest, of those most exhausted and most terrifyingly marked by extreme poverty. Having done so, no stench, no slum can—it seems—disgust them. A Jesuit father from Liège comes to my mind. He has been a volunteer for more than ten years now. When he comes to holy mass with one of the poverty-stricken men he has befriended, people on the adjoining benches are driven away, for the man is disabled and has little means to keep clean and properly dressed. "When I take him in my car, I have a little difficulty breathing myself," says Father de Ghellinck, as in excuse of those who keep their distance in church. As for him, he could not imagine not giving preference to this man above all the other poor in his town. To love the poor, to touch the sick, to embrace the lepers, it is all one. Is this not what Christ wanted to teach us? Is this not also why living in a poverty area and living in the Gospel is all one? For it is, on condition that we be steadfast in prayer.

CHAPTER FOUR

"Lord, If You Are Willing, You Can Make Me Clean"

I hear men talking at one of the ATD Fourth World people's universities. "You see, if I had a house—all right, I don't have one, but let's suppose I had one—well, I would not leave a pal outside" . . . "Let's suppose the boss told me, 'There's no more work for you.' That would have hurt you, right? You would have been sore? Well, that's friendship, when people worry about one another, when they are not indifferent."

Am I wrong in thinking that Jesus spoke no differently? And if He talked like one of them, surely it was not in the manner of some who, speaking to children, adopt what they consider a children's language. He did not take on the role of a pedagogue,

85

using humble folk's language as I have heard students do when going into villages to carry out literacy programmes. Jesus spoke as He was, as one of them. And like them, He did not only use vivid expressions, He also created images by performing gestures and acts.

> *When Jesus came down from the hill,*
> *large crowds followed Him.*
> *Then a man suffering from leprosy came to Him,*
> *knelt down before Him and said,*
> *"Lord, if You are willing,*
> *You can make me clean."*
> *Jesus stretched out His hand and touched him.*
> *"I do want to," He answered. "Be clean!"*
> *At once the man was healed of his disease.*
> *Then Jesus said to him, "Listen!*
> *Don't tell anyone, but go straight to the priest*
> *and let him examine you;*
> *then in order to prove*
> *to everyone that you are cured,*
> *offer the sacrifice that Moses ordered."*
>
> (Matthew 8, 1-4)

Reading such texts, I walk within the Gospel, going from one to the other, lingering in the crowd and seeing Jesus move about. And in doing so, time and again, I feel I touch upon His total genuineness. He is not only true to Himself in His words, His deeds of valour and in the highlights of His teaching, but also in His entire being and His everyday behaviour with those around Him. That is how I see Him by the side of this leper as with so many others: Christ in person, truly Son of God and truly man. The Saviour never cheated; not once did He sacrifice one of these two conditions to the other. Thereby He told us all, but especially He told priests, and religious and lay militants, that it is possible and even perfectly natural and necessary to be all at once a man in poverty taking up the condition of the poorest and a man "not of this world," totally dedicated to the concerns of the Father.

Some, as we said before, chose to see a contradiction there. Belonging to the poorest and at the same time refusing to make use of worldly power on their behalf would somehow be "inhuman." Through His very life, Jesus refutes this. He knows Himself to be the Son of God and He proves that as such He can take any risk, even the risk of total worldly failure. By announcing God to the poor, He has already won. The poorest are already freed as they never will be by any worldly revolution. It is only, however, by following Jesus in His everyday intimacy with those around Him, in His dealing with the most humble without ever making an exhibition of Himself, that we can experience the evangelising of the poor, not as a lesson to be taught, but as a living reality to be shared. Only then do we experience that bringing the Good News means freeing oneself of the powers of intellectual reasoning and money.

Jesus did not just teach us the truth. He said: "I *am* the truth." And to illustrate this He performed gestures of truth. His actions were no more calculated than His words. He did not stage Himself nor produce now a leper, now a paralytic. The way He lived, it was normal that He constantly met lepers.

The path He chose was bound to make Him come across paralytics all the time. And taking now one, now another to bear witness was a matter of course, since His heart, His sensitivity and His eyes could not fail to identify them among the crowds. A Jewish friend told me one day, "Despite the years I have now lived as an American in the United States, I have never gotten rid of the habit of quickly spotting all the Jews in whatever meeting or assembly I find myself." Similarly, Jesus could not but turn instinctively toward His own. He would feel them behind Him when His eyes could not see them. And none knew better than He what privileged witnesses they were of the mercy, the forgiveness, the love of God. The outstanding witnesses of this seemingly insane trust of which the poorest are most capable: "I kneel before You, for You are the Lord and if You are willing, You can make me clean."

On several such occasions, Jesus will repeat that the healing depends on the faith both of the disabled and of the healer. We also know that the countless sick and miserably maimed whom Jesus healed came to Him crawling or carried by near relations. What faith they must have had in Him! The leper at the foot of the mountain is but one among many. Certainly he was one of the most wretched and therefore a choice associate and a perfect witness of the Saviour.

This association of Jesus has always appeared to me an essential subject for meditation. When healing a sick man before our eyes, Jesus shows us a path of truth along which to follow Him. This is why I often bow to the mystery at play between Him and this anonymous leper. Their brief encounter seems to be mentioned almost incidentally, merely one in a long series of such meetings. Yet it is there that the extraordinary miracle happens, "You are healed, You are saved." What secret understanding, what promise, what liberation, what fulfilment of silent hope do we behold?

Throughout the years, I have seen so many men and women place their confidence in just anybody, in anyone who happened to pass by in their slum or settlement and who could not, in the face of so much deprivation, refrain from extending a hand, leaving a little money or promising to undertake some steps on their behalf. The well-off people coming to a poor neighbourhood or a shantytown "to see" are rarely able to bow to so much human suffering, humbly admitting, "I can do nothing, I come from another universe, I am ignorant and unprepared, what could I possibly offer you?" Those who feel themselves totally helpless and useless on such occasions are of the stuff of the just who joined Jesus. But the majority, on the contrary, believe they must offer some spontaneous gesture. They cannot but search in their pockets for some bounty to hand out. They are unable to hold themselves in, to avoid making hasty promises. So they give rise to hopes and certainties out of all proportion: "I just met someone, she even came in to talk to me. She will see to it that I get proper housing!" Such expectations never last and soon bitterness will set in: "I knew all the time she would let me down. . . ." But how could one not cling to those moments of hope which, for a while at least, lift one above the grayness of life?

Was it this insane confidence that prompted the poor to believe the rumour spreading from village to village and all over town: "The lame walk, the blind see, the deaf hear"? Did not another rumour also spread, "He is not a scribe, nor a high priest, He is one of us"? I can imagine the news that would run through poor areas today: "He knows what He is talking about, His own parents have been kicked out and they could never make ends meet. He learned nothing at school, same as our kids. The big shots at the Temple were amazed that He knew so much anyway". . . . That is what I hear families say today when they discuss the Gospel together. Jesus, one of them, cannot but love them since He is the Son of God.

So Jesus is recognised as the one who has only to be willing but also as the one who cannot but be willing, because He knows, He understands. Seeing how the very poor are obliged to live, we realise that this is the only way they can visualise God and His Son. "If He knows what I know, if He understands what we have to go through, if He shares our experience, then He must want what we want. He cannot accept extreme poverty, humiliation, contempt; He must want to put an end to them." Such is the God of the poor, the one who is in their memory, always just under the surface of their thought and existence. Perhaps we too often ignore that in one way or another this God is always present among them. He cannot but be there; deep poverty requires His presence, the presence of a God who takes part in their sorrow at seeing people love one another so little, be so unjust and treacherous. God is not the poor because of what they were taught about Him by sermons or by their elders. He is not present because as children they were told not to forget their prayers. He is there because He cannot be absent if it be true that He refuses to accept the despair of people prevented from recognising themselves as real human beings.

The leper prostrate at the foot of the mountain waiting to be touched by Jesus, believed in Him as no one could who had not endured the same rejection. And we who bow to this scene, which by now has become almost common, realise that doubting the heart of the leper would mean doubting the Lord Himself. It would mean doubting the sincerity of all these human beings asking to be healed, doubting the mystery, the profound brotherhood between Jesus and the poor.

For these poor, for the crowds, Jesus could feel pity. We, however, cannot pity them, or at least we cannot do so in the same way. For our pity is mixed with humility and gratitude. We know that the poor are, throughout the ages, ahead of us on the way to the Kingdom. With their untold sufferings which made it inevitable that they recognise the Son of God, who but they would teach us truly boundless faith and unconditional hope? Without the leper in the Gospel, without the families in extreme poverty today, we would not remain ignorant of a God taught and codified by the Church. But we would only know that part of God which is confined within the walls of our temples, within the limits of our intelligence and our life's experience, which do not always help us reach beyond what is reasonable. We would know a Jesus Christ learnt by heart, as it were, a God of love whom we would tend to see surrounded by safeguards. In the hearts of the very poor, God overflows all barriers, all man-made limits and human reasoning. It is the God of Job, the stubbornly defying faith of Job. It is the God none can imagine, who surpasses all human understanding, the God of men and women too wretched, too deeply submerged in darkness to have an image of Him. And at the same time it is the God who *must* exist, because the darkness inflicted by man is too flagrantly unjust and unbearable for God not to intervene and put an end to it. The leper saying to Jesus, "You can do everything, You and I know that nothing is impossible to You" teaches me hope beyond all reason. He teaches me this God who is love and who like a torrent sweeps away all barriers, hunting down the evils of treachery, exploitation and oppression.

It is of the leper, of all these lepers, these deaf and dumb and blind on the way to Jesus that I think with anxiety when I see so many men and women in poverty who even today turn to priests. If a priest passes by in a poverty area, if they can see that he is a priest, they approach him as they once crowded in on Jesus. Yet, friendly words about the Church have become rare in the streets and settlements where I am at home. The families no longer know the clergy as my mother knew the parish priest who used to visit his parishioners and who knew so well how to listen and to speak to us. He understood as we no longer do today that at some periods in life the only thing that counts is a discreet gesture of help. Still, even now I see people who in times of anguish or at certain turning points in their existence venture to go to the presbytery or stop a priest who happens to come by. They do so in order to obtain a specific aid, for they still see men of God as people disposing of power. But I am certain that they also turn to them for more profound reasons: because they feel it is normal that a priest, a man of God and of prayer, would be in search of the lost sheep as Jesus was. Somehow it seems inconceivable to them that a priest would not descend into the very depths of humanity where people are no longer recognised, where they do not even need to look at one another to know they are of the same miserable condition.

The very poor keep this vision of the priest deep down in their memory, even if he no longer visits them, urging them to register their children for cate- chism classes, encouraging them to love one another despite their countless difficulties. They seem to have kept in mind this image of the parish priest when not much else is left to bind these desperate people to the Church. For what sense of God can our more and more organised Christian community convey to the poor today? Can it continue to develop with them a memory of the Church? Can it echo the Good News among families whose condition it does not share? Echoes from these parishes become ever fainter, as love shared in daily life is replaced more and more by forms of organised participation from which the poor shy away. I often wonder why they hold on to this vision of the priest and the sister consecrated to human suffering and to Jesus the Saviour. This vision is no invention of mine. I am

93

constantly faced with it, wherever I go in areas of extreme poverty. As a priest I am always made to feel at home there, much more so than in other social spheres. It seems as if the hand of the priest has remained the hand of Christ held out to offer bread and forgiveness. Wherever I go, be it to a poor housing settlement in Caen, to a far away village or even a prison in Africa, to a starving hamlet in Guatemala or to a welfare hotel in New York, I can gather around me the people, gather their hands in mine without anyone showing surprise. As if it were natural that around a priest the hands of the outcasts join and no other concern remains but of sharing the bread, the peace, the harmony and the certainty that all people are children of God.

"You can heal me," the crowds said to Jesus, "You can make me clean." Perhaps the exegetes do not always make sufficiently clear to us how universally liberating that purification was at all times and in all cultures. Indeed we know of no people on earth who will not accuse a brother or sister of sin, misconduct, uncleanliness or even witchcraft, casting him out because through infirmity or poverty he has become too heavy a burden on the community. The charge of uncleanliness which entails punishment and even exile has weighed upon the very poor throughout the ages up to our days. Epileptic children or those whose mothers have died in labour, widows who have become useless mouths to feed, poverty-stricken children overcrowding some of our district schools, families who can no longer cope with deprivation, cooped up in slum dwellings,... are they not all condemned without appeal on some pretext of dangerous uncleanliness?

Again, "You, man of God, could cleanse me," is what some mothers mean to say when they come to the parish to ask that their child be baptised. "You at least can do something for me, you cannot refuse to look at me," is also what this man thinks who knocks at the door of the presbytery. In his clumsiness, his nerves on edge, all he can say is, "Could you give me some money? My wife is ill. . ." Should the priest have spared the time, how much could this man have told him, even about his own priesthood!

The poor in the days of Jesus did not need to give lengthy explanations, to make up stories in order to arouse pity and comprehension. "Here I am before you Lord, look at my distress. Heal me, save me." I am filled with anguish at the thought of this tremor of a God of love, of this mad confidence in the heart of the leper. I think of these men who, knocking on the door of my shanty in the Camp for the Homeless in Noisy-le-Grand, tried to say the same thing: "Help me, I know I was wrong. I know I should not get into fights or abuse the police." Was this not their way of saying, "Heal me"? Even when they asked to be granted remission of their sins, they really expected the confirmation of what they deeply felt was God's love: "Go in peace, you are saved, your sins were commensurate with your sorrows, they were the result of all you have had to suffer and could not bear. Go, you are healed, your faith has saved you." Do we think of the loss inflicted on the poor when we priests no longer have the courage to hear their confessions? What means have we kept to reveal to them God, the

Saviour of the crowds?

As we said before, Jesus in no way freed God's children, be they rich or poor, of their responsibilities. But He knew exactly who among them could suffer no other words but these: "Your faith has saved you," because their woe and weakness were at a climax. I am distressed to think that we may not always follow in Christ's footsteps nor resort to His means to be in that state of real communion which allows us to know the moments in which to say: "God is as you thought He was, He is this overflowing love of which you and I can be but a remote reflection. You did well to remind me of that. You knew the truth which I might have forgotten, namely that you are a child of God whom the Father can no more disown than the child can disown his father."

I cannot see the leper before Jesus as an abstract image, the mere symbol of an overpowering faith. He represents an unending questioning of my own daily life: "See how this man reduced to a sub-human condition was able to believe in Jesus. You too are surrounded by people like him. How far have you dared to go to be one of them, capable of an equally intuitive faith, partaking of their faith and knowing how to bear witness to God's love as they sense it?" But if the very poor can sense God, what to think of this other healing, that of the ten lepers of whom only one returned to praise Jesus?

As Jesus made His way to Jerusalem,
He went along the border
between Samaria and Galilee.
He was going into a village,
when He was met by ten men suffering from leprosy.

They stood at a distance and shouted,
"Jesus! Master! Take pity on us!"
Jesus saw them and said to them,
"Go and let the priests examine you."
On the way, they were made clean.
When one of them saw that he was healed,
he came back, praising God in a loud voice.
He threw himself to the ground at Jesus' feet
and thanked Him.
Jesus said, "There were ten men who were healed;
where are the other nine?
Why is this foreigner the only one
who came back to give thanks to God?"
And Jesus said to him,
"Get up and go, your faith has made you well."

(Luke 17, 11-19)

What to think of those nine lepers who were not even grateful for what happened to them? Again the event seems familiar, liable to bring us closer to poor people of all ages. I can think of many sermons I heard drawn from this Gospel text to comment on the world's ingratitude. Even as a child, I was troubled by the interpretations offered. My mother's neighbours too expected her to be grateful. They did not even leave her the time to summon her wits and fully appreciate a kindness done to her, "There now, I am out of the woods! What a relief, how grateful I am!"

What really did happen to the ten lepers? They too must have been stunned by their healing, unable to realise and explain off-hand the miracle that had occurred. Let us imagine the reception they got from the priests and those around them at the synagogue: "Here they are again, these troublesome unclean people. They pretend to be healed by Jesus, no less! When will this man cease meddling in our affairs? Come here, you fellows who claim to be healed! Surely you won't pretend you were miraculously cleansed? Don't think you will get away with that. We'll have to take a closer look, wait and see how things turn out. You cannot possibly think it would suffice that Jesus say to you 'Go and let the priests examine you.' Did He so much as touch you or give you a remedy?"

The lepers must have met with all the more scepticism and irritation, as the rumours of healings greatly troubled dignitaries at the synagogues and the Temple. I have often been faced with similar mistrust, as if good luck were forbidden to the poorest. "There must be something fishy," I was told once, when a very poor family was seen to move from an emergency housing settlement. Overwhelmed with joy, these people were leaving behind the little they had in the way of furniture. The "fishy" thing about their moving was a tiny legacy they had received. But what intrigued some and even roused their indignation was seeing suddenly so happy and independent a family who, for years, had survived on public assistance.

Not only should miracles not happen to the poor, but neither should the poor ever achieve something on their own. Among many mothers who turn each day into a miracle of survival for their children, I remember Madame Rouquier. Her youngest daughter had been placed in foster care. She had achieved unbelievable feats because she had been promised that her daughter would be returned to her if she improved her housing. In her shelter made of gaping slats, she had boarded the holes, scraped the concrete floor and pasted wallpaper where no one could have hoped to make it stick. The welfare inspector in charge of arrangements for the girl's return, on entering the hut, asked but one question, "Who helped you do all this? Did you pay someone?" "I did not," replied the mother. "I did it all myself, I wanted my girl to have her own room and be happy here." The inspector allowed the child to come home, but as she left she turned to me and said, "With these people, one never knows. They're always telling lies."

The very poor always find people who distrust them and have their doubts about whatever happens to them. About a man who has found a job at last, there will always be someone to say, "But will he be able to keep it?" A father who tries to stop drinking will always meet someone who asks, "Are you sure you will make it last?" Of a mother who dreams of seeing her children make good, people will say, "That's all very well, but in the meantime she doesn't even send her kids to school." They are right, but they do not ask themselves whether this mother has what is needed to give the children their breakfast. No one stops to think of the heroism it would require to force the children to leave home on an empty stomach and go to a school where they do not learn. Who will believe that this mother truly dreams of a better future for them?

Beginning with the shepherds whose testimony

was not acknowledged in court and the lepers accused of abuse at the synagogue, up to the very poor of today suspected of "always telling lies," has the word of the outcasts ever been accepted? Why then should we be amazed or indignant at the ungratefulness of the lepers who did not thank Jesus? Should we not rather keep silent as I often had to do, asking myself, "How do I help make the gratitude of the poor shine out, without their being ridiculed, stifled or embittered?"

Ungratefulness, if we choose to call it that, has been my lot since the very first days in the Camp for the Homeless in Noisy-le-Grand. And during the thirty years since, friends have never stopped asking me, "But what results do you obtain? Are these people grateful at least for all the pains that you take?" How could I explain that the better were the results, the less would be the gratitude? This was in fact what happened, at least in the first years. It pained my heart as it pained all volunteers present at that time. But they had the patience, the love, the deep communion needed to understand the countless reasons that made gratitude impossible.

The first of these reasons may well have been the disparaging attitude toward the Voluntariat on the part of the outside services the families had to deal with: "So here you are again, asking for assistance. What then is the point in having those volunteers around you? They thought they were smarter than we are, and there you are, still needing money!" . . . "It's all well and good your volunteers up there. But all I know is that your children missed school again this morning!" Ceaseless comments of this kind caused the families to start insulting the only people who respected them enough to share their lives day and night, giving up the careers and salaries they could have had elsewhere. One civil servant who knew full well that volunteers accepted an income under the public assistance level told families that "these people are paid to serve you." Deeply troubled, the inhabitants of the Camp began to complain, "They are filling their pockets. . . . When my husband was released from the hospital they didn't even go to fetch him. . . . They are of no use to us." Such angers soon dissipated, for in the end no one was proud of them. But they showed how easy it is to confuse the very poorest, to sow doubt in their minds because they have so few certainties, so few people on whom to count.

I do not think that one single family ever was truly misled about the sincerity of this volunteer corps. I believe even less that a single one of the very poor around Jesus was ever really kept from knowing about His true identity. But I know only too well how the better-off can disparage and ridicule their trust. Sometimes they do it out of sheer frustration: "Why do these people win their friendship? Did we not do our best too? Why then do they succeed and take away our clientele?" No doubt the healed lepers met with no more respect and tact at the synagogue. Why would the priests and Pharisees have abstained from sowing doubt in their hearts so as not to shatter their confidence in the only man who had shown them true mercy?

Apart from this constant disparagement, the poorest of course have other reasons not to express their gratitude. When times improve, the very memory of those who helped them keep going during years and years of misery can be unbearable. To remember them means remembering those years of shame when one was made to feel like less than nothing. The very idea of having been unable to pull through by oneself is disheartening. People soon wonder whether they really were less than nothing. Perhaps they still are? "The house I live in, I got it through them," says Mr. Alain, "but don't think I owe them anything!" Forgetting years of humiliation requires more than time. One must have the means to prove to oneself that, away from this Voluntariat which never ran down nor forsook anyone, one is still able to stand up.

I have known families who, once they were resettled and had found work far from any volunteer team, waited several years before getting back in touch. They only sought us out when they could prove they had achieved success or when they had completely failed, sinking back into their former state of poverty.

Finally there is the fear which prevents one from being overwhelmed by gratitude, when the mere fact of having found solutions creates new problems. Be a person ever so poor, sick, illiterate and excluded, everyone achieves some balance which will help him survive. When he sees no possibility to improve his lot, he makes arrangements to put up with it. To him this is a matter of common sense, but some will be quick to blame him: "I told you he is perfectly content the way he is. . . ." Others, unaware of the insult they utter, will assert that he lacks the will to overcome his difficulties. They overlook the talent for survival and resistance present in every human being, and which induces all to invent their very existence and dignity, be their means ever so insufficient.

India and the Moslem countries are not the only ones to ascribe a certain status to the poor and the crippled. A status of poverty, to be sure, the status of a beggar, perhaps, but which nonetheless offers a minimum of security. It has existed over time in all countries. Societies create it or people invent it with the tacit agreement of their entourage. Even Fourth World families today, in a society which no longer recognises extreme poverty, manage to bring about situations which will ensure them a minimum of help, be it that most humiliating of situations where one is passed off as a helpless half-wit. When such a position is suddenly abolished and the habitual status modified, a man and his family may completely lose their bearings. The little security they had laid hold of disappears. It takes fresh courage, new energy and creativity, sometimes an unprecedented daring to begin a new life.

I have witnessed such perplexities and even devastating anguish in men suddenly declared fit to work. I can still recall a manual worker who had his hand severely injured. He gradually settled into the existence of a disabled person which in fact brought him a security that he had never known before. It amounted to an almost negligible financial security, for his pension was insignificant. But he was morally and socially secure at last, since for the first time in his life he was out of work without being criticised

103

for it. Unluckily, surgeons took it into their heads to fit him with a prosthesis. Then the man's martyrdom started all over again, for he was now supposed to return to work, while he was still as illiterate and totally unqualified as before. The idea of having to go back to the unemployment agency week after week was a nightmare to him. I saw this man invent all possible excuses to slow down his rehabilitation, while all around him people unaware of his despair congratulated him on his recovery.

Things are no different for men who in their thirties get the chance to learn to read and write. They suddenly have to face responsibilities they never even imagined and which frighten them. I have seen some of them suffer a real breakdown. Just as I have seen families who lived in slums refuse at the last minute to be moved to more decent quarters. They had suddenly realized that new housing meant a new environment and the loss of the few acquaintances they had. How would they cope without the mutual help among long-standing neighbours, the loans from the lady next door whose husband had managed to find a job? Would another grocer extend them credit? People who leave prison with no prospect of finding work, lodgings, or friendship go through the same ordeal.

Pondering such experiences, I must wonder about these lepers discovering the change for which they were not prepared. "I shall no longer have to keep at a distance, nor have to shout for people to keep away from me. But no one will leave food for me as they used to on the outskirts of the village. How am I going to live here, what can I do, who will want me? Perhaps the priest is right and I'd better wait. Maybe I am not really cured and that might be just as well for me. . . ."

Thinking of these lepers who did not come back to Jesus, I put myself in the place of a man whom I often see at the main entrance of a church in Pontoise. He "panhandles," as the parishioners put it. They all know him, though some seem to ignore him. Others give him a coin or make a disparaging remark. But all this is part of a tacit understanding. At mass, when comes the moment of the kiss of peace, the man enters the church and goes around holding out his hand. No one refuses to shake it. He is part of the ceremony, a poor brother among these people in prayer. He draws no undue attention, simply honours his part of the pact in return for the place he is allowed to hold in this Christian community. The place of a poor man, identified as such.

This of course is no ideal solution. But I often tell myself that thanks to God no one so far has intervened in this fragile equilibrium to disrupt a poor man's existence in the name of who knows what principle. This existence has a meaning, if not in the eyes of men, certainly in the eyes of God.

As for the lepers, Jesus knew what He was doing. He knew the tact and foresight that would be required from the priests and the community to have those who had been condemned to slow death return among the living. He asked about those who did not return to praise God, but He never accused them of ingratitude. He knew the hearts and lives of the

105

excluded far too well to feel Himself cheated. He must have felt sorrow, a pain which foreshadowed all the suffering he was going to bear up to the final sacrifice. But He never said the poorest had forsaken Him. He knew their faith and also the frailty of their opinions when it came to holding their own in the face of those who oppressed and belittled them. His severity with the rich, the Pharisees and all others who prevented the poor from entering the Kingdom was unquestionable. To me, the nine lepers who never came back are part of that reality of the Pharisees barring poor people's access to God. The question, "Were they not healed?" is addressed to us all.

Christ and the lepers yesterday, Christ and the outcasts today, are a mystery on which we shall never finish meditating.

CHAPTER FIVE

"Nor Shall You Be Called Teacher. . ."

Searching for Jesus among those who surround Him day after day, smelling the crowd, our ears filled with its cries and with the high-pitched voices of the poor who become restive; being jostled and touched by them who have eyes only for Him and who quarrel, "Leave me some room!", "Don't push like that, I was here first." Following the awful procession of the diseased bodies, meeting the blind eyes of people groping past us in panic: "Where is He? How will I find Him in this mob?" Searching for the Lord in the very depths of human suffering, there where it piles up in the lives not only of individuals, but of an entire population, to such an extent that rescue can come only from a miracle, from a Saviour. . . . Searching ever further and deeper, knowing that whatever point we reach, Jesus will already have left because He too is searching for ever more wretched human beings, right up to those very poorest among the poor who wait for Him in Jerusalem. . . .

The other day I stopped in the middle of the marketplace of Bossangoa. A marketplace which had nothing in common with those visited by tourists in Abidjan, Dakar, Bouaké, or even along the road from Cotonou to Abomey. This is a market for the very poor who have but few goods to trade in tiny quantities: a few pancakes, matches bundled in fives, a handful of mangoes. . . . All the people of the little town seemed to be assembled there, including the healed lepers, who kept their distance—an ocean of human misery, of very poor people exploited by people hardly less poor than themselves: Haoussa traders, believed therefore to be rich. I wondered once again whether this was not the crowd as it had surrounded Christ. These men and women assembled in a market which reflected their poverty, with colourless stalls, deprived of handicraft and of lush mounds of produce of the soil, would they not be the first sought out by Christ if He passed through Africa today? It struck me once more how much I would always need to make sure and never cease my searching.

It is not for me to invent Jesus' entourage, the atmosphere around Him, the sick He chose, according to my personal preferences. But how can I understand the Lord in His great moments and crucial lessons, how can I imagine Him unless I am immersed ever deeper in the reality of His daily existence? How can I be close to Him in prayer and love Him, unless I try to be with those He chose as His nearest, the first to experience His tenderness, patience and mercy?

I must not trump up this humanity He loved so much. As I said before: Jesus does not leave us this liberty. Neither do I think that He expects us all to conduct scholarly historical and sociological studies, comparing yesterday's poor to today's. But I profoundly believe that He invites us to meditate while going to and fro between the Gospel and the poorest of our own time. "Lord, how deep was Your pity but also Your sorrow when seeing these lepers, so covered with pustules and rags, knowing Your own too well not to realise that nine out of ten would not come back. . . . I offer You my sorrow, Lord, for those families out of work who had nothing but rags to put on their backs and who yet left us in peace once they knew that, together, we had found some means to save their children. I offer you my pain for all those parents who never came back because they had been put up to ridicule for having been helped by a priest or a handful of volunteers: 'It's all very well, you and your priest! Now all you have to do is go back to ask him for new housing!'"   ·

All this came to my mind in the midst of the crowd which jostled me in Bossangoa. I thought of the humble nuns not far from there, on the outskirts of town, caring for the lepers, helping women in excruciating labour, their bodies distorted by too much bending. Of these nuns it will never be said that they contributed to the development of the country. Some will even disparage them for doing nothing "to promote structural change." As I heard a compatriot say, "They are not like those nuns in Brazil, who found militant communities and study land reform." He was right no doubt, but between the militant communities in Brazil and the leprosy in Bossangoa, what would be the choice of Jesus? Where does He turn in the Gospel? To a village full of energy where politically aware peasants organise to purchase their seeds on a cooperative basis? Or to a community where harsh conditions have rendered relations bitter and ruthless, where the search for a Saviour is desperate, a community where lepers cannot rejoice for being healed? Would He perhaps go to both, but linger a while longer in the second?

Would Christ today be seen in the streets or the squares where money changes hands and people are absorbed in their own business? Or would He be in the market of Bossangoa, where faces sweat with malaria ("I've got a touch of flu"), where foreigners control most trade, where people wear "chosen" clothing rather than the traditional "pagne" or "boubou", "choosing" among second-hand t-shirts and jeans shipped in bulk from Europe and heaped in a jumble on the bare soil? Pushing further into the country, would Jesus take the passable roads leading to the villages where peasants are organised? He would, no doubt, but would He not choose, in preference to all others, the track to Nana Bakassa, Kuki and Markunda, a little more cracked and difficult to use after each rainy season? There, people are slow to smile since malnutrition, fever and amoebae have worn out their bodies. Exhausted peasants stretch out their hands, make an effort to get on their feet and then give up. One would think these hamlets to be

110

inhabited only by children and old people, so heavy is the toll of fatigue each year. Here the average life span is barely forty years, and the younger and more energetic flee to a more mild climate.

It is not in this border region where refugees from over the river come and go, reducing to nothing the already sparse resources, that we shall see a World Bank programme. The World Health Organisation, UNICEF, the International Development Agency. . . no one here has been able to tell us for what these names stand. People have at times been bestowed with bags of grain marked "WFP", but they do not know what these initials mean. It was long ago, anyway. "Perhaps people out there don't know that we still exist?" As for the international non-governmental organisations, "What do you mean by that? We don't know them, they don't come here. We only know the fathers and the good sisters. . ."

To be sure, in order to meditate better on the Gospel, we shall not think first of going to the dam built on the Senegal River. Might we rather turn to the south of Central Africa where new efforts are spent on improving the meagre cotton crop? Wherever we go, we must remember that beyond the areas where development is furthered, remain these regions left with only "the fathers and the good sisters," whose true mission is to proclaim: "Your faith has saved you, your soul will not be eaten by witches, your soul will live." Your faith has saved you, because you had nothing else left. No dam rose against your skyline to give you some hope, and you never met with a passing cotton expert explaining how you could

111

double your crop. The Church did not take the wrong road when going there. Is this not the very reason why for some time now, she has been discredited by those who cannot understand that economic efficiency is not the last word? The ATD Fourth World team in that same forlorn part of Africa meets with similar disparagement: "Why waste their efforts with a population unable to organise cooperative action and put in a collective request for fertilisers? No doubt the volunteers are going to do as did the good sisters, teaching the women to knit!" Indeed, the sisters had done just that and it had shown their sharp perception of a people constantly deprived of its cotton, the fruit of their labour in the sweltering heat. It had required carrying the burden of life together, to sense what the hands of these women were waiting for: to spin and turn their cotton into handicraft themselves, so as to give colour and beauty to their bodies and huts, to their environment and religious rites. Do the agents of development programmes in the least advanced countries take the time for such communion with the people as did Jesus, and as do these nuns? The time to develop common sensitivity: "I have lived, suffered and hoped with you long enough to feel what you feel." The time of the thirty years of the Lord's life on earth led Him to this unique moment which only a communion of that quality could make possible:

A woman who had suffered
from severe bleeding for twelve years
came up behind Jesus
and touched the edge of His cloak.
She said to herself,

"If only I can touch His cloak, I will get well."
Jesus turned round and saw her, and said,
"Courage, my daughter!
Your faith has made you well."
At that very moment the woman became well.

(Matthew 9, 20-22)

She was behind Him, making herself inconspicuous, bending to touch His robe. Anyone else would have followed on his way without noticing her. Anyone else but Christ who felt the people's suffering as His own and could not but sense it in each person coming near.

Jesus was good to her, the Gospel says. He singled her out, contrary to law and customs which would have Him send away this impure, useless woman. All this is for us to meditate upon. But are we not struck with wonder, first of all, by the fact that Jesus knew she was there behind Him, feeling her anxiety and tremulous hope? Twelve years of haemorrhage that nothing could stop, twelve years of exhaustion, and above all, twelve years of contempt for being untouchable, impure. "Do not come near me..." Even before seeing her, Christ could feel what her entourage had refused to consider: the burden of twelve years of solitude and pain.

We must not forget that Jesus had been called elsewhere. He and His disciples had on their minds the daughter of a prominent man who had just died. This is how meetings and healings often come about in the Gospel. Jesus, His attention seemingly elsewhere, on His way to attend to an important matter, stops short because a pain too deep to be suffered crosses His path. Even His disciples would have passed on their way, as we so often do ourselves. "They have no time for us, we are of no concern to them," the Fourth World families say, and they add: "They are always in meetings." Jesus Christ could not hurry on that way. He was forever at the mercy of the pains that broke the most humble. He could not avoid seeing them, nor hasten His steps, saying, "It can't be helped, I'll see to this some other time." This woman's sorrow was His own and He felt her anguish before she spoke.

The evangelist Luke, intent on giving more details, adds that Jesus felt her hand and therefore turned to her. But that does not dispel the mystery of the communion between Jesus and the woman. Peter gets impatient, "Lord, these people push and grasp at You." Then why worry about one more hand which tries to touch Him? Luke says: "Because some power compelled Him." But then, what was this "power," unless it were the communion with the pain of this woman yet unseen? To the mind of one cautious exegete, the power in question is "an energy that can operate independently of Christ's will, although He is aware of it."* Would this not describe precisely the sensitivity that became a part of Christ's personality through a life of sharing with the poor and despised of Galilee?

Again, I think of Africa and Brother Albin Descombes, passing by a hut where a woman was sitting in the shade. She did not say a word, nor call for his atten-

*Traduction oecumenique de la Bible, New Testament, page 222, note q.

tion, but only looked at him. What then happened between those two to make Brother Albin suddenly stop and turn to this woman hidden in the shade? "You are not well. Let me leave this with you. Take two of them now and two more tonight."

I feel I should never stop meditating on Christ's unfailing sensitivity. How can we develop it in ourselves? While Brother Albin was on his way through this village, another European was in Africa on quite different business. As a commissioner of the European Economic Community, he was inspecting a dam financed by Europe to improve irrigation in a desert region. He too was a man of integrity, intent on combatting poverty. But what were his chances of feeling the desperation this very project had brought to the landless? What was he allowed to see, whom did he meet? Our present-day structures have made him a prisoner of technocracy, unable even to silence his own technical reasoning in order to listen to the men and women in whose lives he interferes, unable to allow himself to be disturbed in his technical planning by people of flesh and blood. As a civil servant of high rank, surrounded by experts, he may have met with some organised farmers, touched the high-quality rice they now produce, looked at sophisticated evaluations of maximum crop increase. But who helped him feel the silent sorrow or meet the eyes of those landless men who, because of the dam, lost their last chance to hire out the labour of their now useless arms?

When we talk about the sensitivity of Christ taking upon Himself the anguish of the poor which escapes the awareness of the wealthy, when we discuss Christians' responsibility to take on the role of watchmen, some people turn the issue: "So, you're against big works of development?" This of course is not the point. The determination to harness the forces of our environment does us credit. But did not Jesus remind us that the greater control for some is often achieved at the expense of others? It rarely serves to save all from exploitation and dependency. On the contrary, new powers in new hands most often mean new oppression. And a dam in the heart of a parched country means immense power. The water which suddenly flows more plentiful has not necessarily cleansed people of their rivalries, nor quenched their thirst for influence. Jesus does not expect us to oppose the construction of dams, but to be close both to the oppressed who will make no profit and to the beneficiaries, so that all may receive their rightful part. Our concern is not about irrigation projects, nor even about the unequal distribution of their profits. We question those who surround a high-ranking official and prevent him from hearing the complaint of the poorest and from meeting them face to face. Would these experts be the Pharisees of development? The commissioner was not even allowed to meet people who would speak on behalf of the poorest. He wasn't given the time to sit with them. And the din of technocracy was too loud for him to hear those who in that region had tried to follow the Lord, intent on preventing new injustice.

But there is more to learn from Christ's healing of the bleeding woman. By associating with the impure

116

and the dishonoured who can only jeopardise His prestige, Jesus truly compromises Himself. We could have known, since we witnessed His commitment during the temptation in the desert. But we could not imagine then how far His renunciation would go. As we probe deeper into the Gospel, we discover increasingly definite and disconcerting signs. In His refusal of worldly prestige, Jesus does not limit Himself to sharing life with the "honest poor," the "new poor," or the deserving ones who are no danger to the respectability of a community. But was it necessary that He go as far as associating with the cursed ones? In fact, Christ does not bother to answer this question, which is on the minds of the apostles. The answer is there in His very life. It clearly says, "How would I be totally obedient, how would I ever reach Golgotha and the Cross of the humiliated and of the damned, if I did not, from the beginning, follow their path, share their lives and their hopes?" This is what we learn from His daily gestures:

> When evening came,
> people brought to Jesus many who had demons
> in them.
> Jesus drove out the evil spirits with a word
> and healed all who were sick.
> He did this
> to make what the prophet Isaiah had said
> come true,
> "He Himself took our sickness
> and carried away our diseases."
> (Matthew 8, 16-17)

Must we invent limits to that taking responsibility for infirmities and diseases? Could Jesus take up the infirmity of the possessed, without taking up their state of rejection, the horror and fright they aroused everywhere? In the evening, all the townspeople come to ask Him to leave. . . Could He take on the suffering of the lepers, of the bleeding woman, without sharing the stigma attached to their diseases?

Jesus answers these questions first, not by lecturing, but through His way of life. And it was certainly not only His teaching that brought Him to the Cross. He was crucified not only for His proclamation to be the Messiah and His acts of mercy. It was His total identification with the rejected, His choosing them as confidants and messengers, that sealed His fate at Golgotha. Far from provoking only theological controversies, His teachings and life overturned the worldly order. "But many who now are first will be last, and many who now are last will be first." (Matthew 19, 30) Christ in fact realised this prophecy by His very choice of friends and companions. The Kingdom was already there, in all truth. And it was inacceptable then, as it is now.

Not long ago, Madame Hélène Monnier had to learn this. The mayor of her town had asked her to establish a liaison between families in extreme poverty and municipal social services. It did not take her very long to discover just to what extent the needs and expectations of the excluded upset established systems. Public Assistance, for instance, turned out to be ill-adjusted to households totally deprived of

118

income and whose child allowances were late. Soon it also became clear that large families could in no way find housing through the Social Resettlement Programme, provisions having been made for households with only one or two children. Other difficulties arose with regard to school attendance of retarded children and providing jobs to unemployed workers who had not qualified for any benefits for several years. All these problems came to light because, for the first time, the Fourth World families, through Hélène Monnier, could speak for themselves rather than having to wait for others to identify their needs.

In fact, living up to their legitimate expectations turned out to require basic changes in current ways of enforcing human rights. It meant modifying the entire social legislation. That of course was out of the question. No wonder Mme. Monnier soon became an undesirable intermediary in the eyes of the civil servants at the Town Hall. She was treated, at best, as a lady bountiful for Fourth World families, her presence with public authorities becoming not only useless but counter-productive.

Hélène Monnier had done no more than apply these words of Jesus, "Nor shall you be called 'Teacher,' because your one and only teacher is the Messiah." (Matthew 23, 10) A truly intolerable revision of established hierarchies, which Jesus is going to effect once more by choosing a Samaritan woman as His first confidant on a question normally reserved for the most learned among scholars and priests.

Jacob's well was there,
and Jesus, tired out by the journey,
sat down by the well.
It was about noon.
A Samaritan woman came to draw some water,
and Jesus said to her,"Give me a drink of water."
His disciples had gone into town to buy food.
The woman answered, "You are a Jew,
and I am a Samaritan—
so how can You ask me for a drink?"
For Jews will not use
the same cups and bowls that Samaritans use.
Jesus answered, "If only you knew what
God gives
and who it is that is asking you for a drink,
you would ask Him and He would give you
life-giving water."
"Sir," the woman said,
"You haven't got a bucket,
and the well is deep.
Where would You get that life-giving water?
It was our ancestor Jacob
who gave us this well;
he and his sons and his flocks all drank from it.
You don't claim to be greater than Jacob, do you?"
Jesus answered, "Whoever drinks this water
will be thirsty again,
but whoever drinks the water that I will give him
will never be thirsty again.
The water that I will give him
will become in him a spring
which will provide him with life-giving water
and give him eternal life."

"Sir," the woman said, "give me that water!
Then I will never be thirsty again,
nor will I have to come here to draw water."
"Go and call your husband," Jesus told her,
"and come back."
"I haven't got a husband," she answered.
Jesus replied, "You are right when you say
you haven't got a husband.
You have been married to five men,
and the man you live with now
is not really your husband.
You have told me the truth."

"I see you are a prophet, sir," the woman said.
"My Samaritan ancestors worshipped God
on this mountain,
but you Jews say that Jerusalem
is the place where we should worship God."
Jesus said to her, "Believe me, woman,
the time will come when people will not
worship the Father
either on this mountain or in Jerusalem.
You Samaritans do not really know
whom you worship;
but we Jews know whom we worship,
because it is from the Jews that salvation comes.
But the time is coming, and is already here,
when by the power of God's spirit,
people will worship the Father as He really is,
offering Him the true worship that He wants.
God is spirit, and only by the power of His spirit
can people worship Him as He really is."
The woman said to Him,
"I know that the Messiah will come,

and when He comes, He will tell us everything."
Jesus answered, "I am He,
I who am talking with you."

(John 4, 6-26)

The event is certainly far beyond our comprehension, as it was beyond the disciples', too stunned to question Jesus: "What are You trying to do?" or "Why on earth do You speak to her?" What then was so stunning as to silence His companions, usually so quick to assail their Master with questions?

Here is a Samaritan woman coming to draw water. She comes around noon, to remain unseen, no doubt, since it is not the hour kept by the other women, who go to the well together. A Samaritan woman despised even by her own, and certainly very poor. For no upright man would have taken for a companion a woman who has already lived with so many others. An impure woman, to be sure, twofold, threefold impure to the Jew Jesus. How much more wonderful, then, is the conversation that follows. In my experience, only the very poorest have this manner of being on an equal footing with people of high rank. Those who claim a status, be it ever so modest, do not dare behave with such artless ease. The very poor often confabulate and redesign reality to survive, to wheedle some assistance or to fend off a menace. They could not live and maintain a pretence to dignity otherwise. But they do not have the self-complacency and self-consciousness of those who, having reached a certain level of prestige, must see to it that they stay there or even climb higher. I have seen fathers in extreme poverty receive a Head of State in their homes on New Year's Day. I have seen women have discussions with a Minister, and a whole group of families take supper at the Ministry of Finance. They were artless in the best sense of the word.

The Evangelist John discloses that same artlessness. Of course, Jesus' own personality calls for it. Christ can always be recognised by His simplicity. I see Him so much at ease, so devoid of the awkwardness which often overcomes the well-off when they meet a poverty-stricken person. A woman marked by the fate of the Samaritan has misery and contempt written all over her. I have thought of her so often, believing I saw her in the fleeing silhouette of a woman carrying her pail at dusk to the only common outhouse in the Camp for the Homeless in Noisy-le-Grand. I felt I recognised her too in this mother stepping out to fetch water with an air of defying the world, looking neither right nor left, but hastening her step as to avoid being mocked. I never felt more shame and suffering than in these women, sometimes only girls, bracing themselves in advance against jeers and leers. I never felt more pain and pity myself, than when I crossed their path.

The Samaritan woman, to me, must have been Héléna. She too would try to sneak into the neighbourhood unseen, when she came home a little tipsy. She would slip up the stairs or hide behind a cellar door to avoid the scorn and haughtiness of the other women. Héléna was not only very poor, she was also Polish. I never forgot the reproving looks I got from her neighbours when, one May Day, at a friend's request, I came to bring her a sprig of lily-of-the-valley. I am sure they mistrusted the priest I was: "So even he is seduced by that tramp?" Like so many other women too poor to defend themselves, Héléna had had several husbands. She had been too weak to keep at bay the last one, who beat her from time to time. The mother of three children, her life had been hard to bear, swathing her in a daze of sadness. She was taken to be an "easy" woman. And visiting her with lily-of-the-valley meant compromising myself, as I could plainly see in the neighbours' eyes.

For having jeopardised my prestige, Héléna thanked me by speaking about God. She first talked to me about her childhood, her youth between Poland and France, her parents dying during deportation, the days of hunger and promiscuity in furnished rooms in post-war Paris. Then she said, almost complaining, "And yet I am a Christian, I would like to find God and love Him." Was it the Samaritan woman I heard, "Where should I go to worship Him?" Héléna said, "I cannot go to church. Could you imagine me in church?" To me that was precisely the point. How could I *not* imagine her in church and long to see her there? But Héléna insisted, "Don't tell me any tales, I know what I'm worth. Just look at my swollen face." "That's of no importance," I argued. "What counts is that you go see the Holy Virgin. Around Mary, you'll find other women praying and you'll find Jesus." "I have the Holy Virgin here," Héléna replied. "Look at my little statue. And I also pray, but only when the children are out. I pray when I get really frightened, but I am too ashamed to ask Jesus as I was taught as a kid: Have mercy on me. For what must He think of me? But still, I believe He hears and forgives me." Thanks to the Samaritan woman, I could tell Héléna she was entirely right. Then and there she sank to her knees, reciting the Lord's Prayer with me.

This was just a small event in an ordinary priest's existence. But how extraordinary was the intimacy woven between a Fourth World mother today and the Samaritan woman chosen by Jesus. I imagine the spontaneous companionship that would have sprung up between the two at the well, the atmosphere in which both could go directly to the heart of the matter. At the well, Jesus did not ignore the woman's wretchedness nor her state as a sinner, but He put them in their proper perspective. They became the starting point for a clarification which was, it seems, as important to Christ as it was to the woman. We must remember that, at that time, the disciples of John were arguing with those of Jesus. Will Jesus Himself push simplicity so far as to share this question with a woman totally ignorant of theological debate? She knows no more than is thought fit for the ears of the humble: "You shall do this. . . . You shall not do that. . . . You shall worship on this mountain, and not as do the Jews in Jerusalem." How could Christ think of going to the heart of the matter with her?

But this is exactly what He does. Always equal to Himself, He does not set up this meeting or adapt His words for some pedagogical purpose. As before all the other encounters we are given to contemplate, I rest in admiration before the inevitableness of the exchange by the well. Jesus and the Samaritan woman being who they are, both with their own preoccupations, their conversation could not have taken any other course. We can love this Jesus, fully alive and about His business. He doesn't tell us the truth; He lives it before our eyes. He *is* the Truth.

No wonder, then, that the Samaritan woman learns before the doctors of Law, and even before the disciples, the quality of worship God would expect of humanity from then on. Jesus does not temporarily put off the crucial issues of the day, to take a little time off with a sinner. He confides a crucial issue to her. And from this confidante, He makes a messenger: "Come, see the man who told me everything I ever did! Could this be Christ?" The other Samaritans will not fail to put her in her place eventually: "We no longer believe just because of what you said. Now we have heard for ourselves." But what does it matter? The difficulty to admit that someone smaller than us has taught us something seems inherent to human nature. What could the poorest possibly have to teach us? Nevertheless, the Samaritan woman remains the messenger Jesus chose. Even as He chose the woman cured of her bleeding and the leper who returned to declare his faith to Jesus and the crowd!

All these personalities—for they are great personalities thus making their way through the Gospel—are in the image of Jesus, all at once messengers and living examples of the message: "I am forgiven. I am the one who no longer dared show her face in the house of worship, but who prayed to God in her heart." Blessed messengers to whom Jesus says, and who will say in their turn: God is not in the first place a theological issue, God is love. Messengers chosen by Christ to tell us even more: "If your theologies are no longer accessible to the poor, and if they confine you to arguments among experts, they no longer concern God." We could still misunderstand in the case of the Samaritan woman. Did Jesus not reduce the problem to its simplest form just to make Himself understood by an ignorant woman? But Jesus never did indulge in what we would call "extension work" today. He elucidated essentials, and I sincerely believe that what was essential was accessible, not only to the heart, but also to the intelligence of the one who listened. Her own intelligence of human existence could fully embrace His teaching, just as the intelligence the poorest had of life itself could fully embrace His healings.

The maimed, the blind, the humble woman ill for twelve years, the disgraced woman of Samaria. . . , none of them was, nor ever could be a theologian. We are told that, by taking them for companions, Jesus showed us His mercy. I believe that He was doing much more. The Samaritan woman running to the village, "Come, everyone, come see!" was by no means a blind tool. The woman who was in the habit of going to the well when no one would see her, did not rush to her neighbours and show herself as she was, unthinkingly. "Come see a man who told me everything I've ever done!" And she adds, "Could this be Christ?" She already believed that a Messiah called Christ would come to "tell all." The remission of sins, love, the living water that would quench thirst forever, the importance of what people believe in their hearts and minds, she was fully prepared to hear about it all.

And what if we followed the wrong theology, or perhaps the wrong theologians? What if we had at last to rediscover the men and women who hold the essentials of all knowledge on God, no matter what formal reasoning the highly educated may draw from them? What if we re-read our theologies as we re-read the Gospel here, the Gospel as experienced by the poorest? What countless hours and years, what ages of meditation on these humble witnesses of the life and person of Christ there are to be rediscovered and assembled! For there has been no single moment in the Church's history when this meditation has not been going on somewhere. The tragedy, the true poverty of our time is that we have let this meditation slip through the fingers of the Church so often. There is no place where its memory is kept alive — the memory of the crippled and the lame, of the little woman shrivelled by illness and painfully bending to touch the hem of Christ's garment; the memory of the Samaritan woman whose heart leapt, "Come, everyone, here is a man. . ." and the memory of all those who let themselves be nourished by the life, the intelligence of the heart and mind of the most humble, of those loved by the Lord with good reason!

The Church, our tender but wasteful Holy Mother who possesses such jewels, (the tears and thoughts and hopes of the poorest and of those who seek them out), lets such riches slip through her fingers.

CHAPTER SIX

Gestures Which Restore Honour

One evening, during common prayers among families in extreme poverty in the Paris area, we discussed the Samaritan woman. "And to think that Jesus told only that woman!" Madame Larmand exclaimed. Angèle Larmand is the mother of five children. Her husband, who is illiterate and has no professional skills, is not physically strong enough to do the work he is offered. Yet, he is not exhausted enough to register as sick or disabled. He is classified as an unemployed worker who does not qualify for legal benefits. Both parents are treated as ignorant people wherever they go. Social workers and officials at the employment agency hardly take the pains to explain to them their situation and rights. "It's too complicated for them to understand. Anyway she is the only one who can fill out the forms and even she is not good at it!" This is what a district employee says, and the local schoolteachers do not think differently. "I would like my children to learn," says Mme. Larmand with a sigh. "Look what it did to my husband to have no education. I have tried to talk to the schoolmistress, but she always sends me packing. 'Don't you worry, Madame, we take care of them,' is what she says. Don't parents have a right to know?" Mme. Larmand, who really wants to be a good mother, went one evening with a neighbour to a parent-teacher meeting. She understood nothing and did not dare ask questions. She never went again.

"And Jesus said that only to her," she repeats. "He knew that she would understand and go tell the others." Little by little, Mme. Larmand discovers that the Gospel is replete with important messages entrusted to people profoundly despised by their associates. Sometimes the messages take on an almost confidential character: "In your sorrow, you stopped me on my way. Now you are saved and I have entrusted you with a unique message. . . ." Even more beautifully, the message is sometimes elucidated with the very person who came to Jesus. This is what happened to the woman from Canaan.

> Jesus left that place
> and went off to the territory of Tyre and Sidon.
> A Canaanite woman who lived
> in that region came to Him.
> "Son of David," she cried out,
> Have mercy on me!

My daughter has a demon
and is in a terrible condition."
But Jesus did not say a word to her.
His disciples came to Him and begged Him,
"Send her away!
She is following us and making all this noise!"
Then Jesus replied,
"I have been sent only to those lost sheep,
the people of Israel."
At this, the woman came and fell at his feet,
"Help me, sir!" she said.
Jesus answered, "It is not right
to take the children's food
and throw it to the dogs."
"That's true, sir," she answered,
"but even the dogs eat the leftovers
that fall from their masters' table."
So Jesus answered her,
"You are a woman of great faith!
What you want will be done for you."
And at that very moment, her daughter was
>*healed.*

(Matthew 15, 21-28)

What delights the families, and me, again and again, is finding Christ always entirely participating in the life of the poor. The idea that the poor should participate *in our projects* is contemporary. It seems to stem from a misunderstanding about the kind of rapprochement which is needed between the rich and the poor. Who should inspire whom? Who holds the life experience and essential thinking necessary to remake our world, our institutions, our

131

religion and faith?

Jesus does not organise participation, He *is* communion, and from the conversations we have the joy of witnessing, wondrous light is bound to spring, a light which stuns us, precisely because the poor are not restricted to participation in a thinking that was primarily developed without them. They do, in fact, create original thought themselves on the very basis of their unique experience of extreme poverty and exclusion. Such thought inevitably surprises the affluent. I feel that this is part of the logic of the Gospel. Yet many commentaries seem to say the contrary.

In the case of the Samaritan woman, for instance, it will be said: "Precisely because He is a Jew and because He is faced with a sinner, a heretic and a woman, He is going to put Himself in a position to ask her something, rather than being the one who gives alms. There are many lessons to learn from this: the more superior one feels to somebody, the more one must place oneself in the position of a beggar and of one who has to ask for things." I find this remark in *L'Aujourd'hui des Evangiles* by Jean-Louis Barreau.

Jesus, seen as a pedagogue, "placing Himself in the position of a beggar" for the occasion? Should we forget that He was thirsty and that He had nothing on Him in the way of alms? Is it then too difficult to face Jesus as a very poor man, completely natural and on an equal footing with the most humiliated among people? I have said before that representing Jesus as someone inventing the part and techniques of a pedagogue does an injustice to His person. But it also involves the risk of a dangerous misapprehension about the paths to be taken in order to follow Him. We see Him in the Gospel, now harassed and sighing or even losing His temper, now joyful and prompting the crowd to feast. We see Him so much like the poor, all at once indignant and showing it, and overflowing with tenderness; all at once delicate and stunningly straightforward as a man brought up in worldly manners for thirty years could not have been. Jesus exemplifies a man from a poor people, devoid of false pretensions. Whoever has lived in poor areas recognises Him with immense joy. Even Matthew, the evangelist sparing of words and ever anxious to present us the Master, does not obliterate the figure of the poor and simple man who behaves artlessly with His own. Is not the very mystery of the Son of God made man precisely there?

We should not, in any case, deprive the encounter with the Canaanite woman of all its liveliness and flavour by turning it into a pedagogical exercise. We have the privilege of witnessing a mutual reprimand, full of spontaneity and temper on both sides. The woman shouts, and what is more, she shouts at a foreigner! That in itself is not the behaviour of a nicely brought-up woman. She is obviously poor, she shouts and probably gesticulates as do all very poor people when they feel they cannot make themselves understood. Her manner becomes very embarrassing to the point of upsetting the disciples who have gone through quite a few disconcerting encounters already. "Do as she asks and she will leave us in peace. . ." But this is not the style of Jesus. If there are things to be said, let them be said outright.

With Christ, the very poor can really talk, argue and even persuade Him, which would be unthinkable with the scribes and the doctors of law. Also, the poor never seem to miss an opportunity of doing so. And here we see once again a woman going home with a unique message which she herself helped to formulate. Before God, there can be no differentiation according to nationality, no worldly formality can stand in the way. No human being can be brought down to the level of a dog and receive only crumbs. "I am a woman of Canaan, yet my daughter is healed as if she were of the House of Israel."

One day I thought I saw the Canaanite woman pass my way, her child in her arms. Actually it was Madame Pimort acting in collusion with other women of the Camp in Noisy-le-Grand. They had heard that the mayor was coming down and they intended to meet him. It was winter and they were badly dressed. They came up in a somewhat disorderly way, talking loudly and gesticulating: "Our children have a right to housing where they won't be dehydrated in summer and cold to the bones in winter. We may be living in this Camp, but we are not dogs, Mr. Mayor."

The Canaanite woman, was she not also Mme. Parmentier, going from door to door to collect signatures for a petition for better housing? Her husband had been out of work for a long time by then and she had no coal or firewood to stoke her stove. She picked up wood wherever she could find it in the neighbourhood. She picked it up, but she did not steal it. "We may be living in the Camp, but we are not dogs."

"We may be living in this wretched place. . . ." "I may be a Canaanite woman. . . ." As a man said to me again recently, "For God, it cannot matter." He was coming home empty-handed. "Nowadays in Paris, rubbish bins are out, but they all carry locks. Where am I to go now?" After a moment of silence, he added: "For God, it cannot matter that I live here. For the mayor, yes, but not for God. If it did, God would not exist."

For Mr. Radier, God must exist. Because there must exist a God who will not discriminate as do the housing authorities. "So, you live in the 'Moulin Neuf.' Perhaps, you'd better come by some other day, sir!" If Jesus were to pass through the poverty-stricken "Moulin Neuf" settlement, where more than half the lodgings are declared insanitary and bricked up, Mr. Radier would be among the crowd proclaiming Him the Son of God. Mr. Radier would go and show Him his swollen knee without hesitation, certain that he would henceforth be able to distribute his advertisement leaflets from door-to-door without the atrocious pain he now has to suffer in order to earn a little money. Mr. Radier would have the faith that had all these men and women who were moulded through and through by unending pain and whom Jesus met because His way was bound to pass among them. Perhaps Mr. Radier would have been among those He chose to become His witnesses and messengers. Sometimes they became unique messengers to whom Jesus left full responsibility for reporting what they had learned. Sometimes they became the co-actors in front of a wide audience. In any case, they were privileged witnesses of a very special intimacy

135

with Christ.

We find it hard to leave these blessed people. Let us linger a while still with this paralytic who—lo and behold!—is lowered down on his stretcher through the roof (Mark 2, 1-12). How poor and desperate they must have been, he and those who carried him, to act with such lack of consideration! What well-bred, thoughtful neighbour would have dared show such insistence? "We must imagine a Palestinian house with only one storey and a roof made of wood and mud," the commentary of the "Traduction Oecuménique" of the Bible tells us with candour. Perhaps we should first of all imagine the impatience of those very poor people, their nerves on edge, always prone to take hasty and often blundering action, usually breaking more things than they can mend. Jesus has eyes only for their eagerness, their certainty that He will understand. I feel sure that they will have been the very first to grasp the meaning of these words, "My son, your sins are forgiven." Like all these desperate people, they must have been longing with all their hearts to hear these words, in a world which never ceased to tell them they were a nuisance. There was not only the paralytic at Jesus' feet, there were these four men on the roof, already much confused about their own daring and afraid they would be driven away any minute. It was certainly not by chance that the Lord's first words were, "You are forgiven."

Then Christ takes the man on the stretcher and his four friends to witness a solemn and truly majestic gesture:

"I will prove to you, then,
that the Son of Man has authority on earth
to forgive sins."
So he said to the paralysed man,
"I tell you, get up, pick up your mat and go home!"
While they all watched,
the man got up, picked up his mat
and hurried away.
They were all completely amazed
and praised God, saying:
"We have never seen anything like this!"

(Mark 2, 10-12)

What great honour was thus done to a man tra-
ditionally considered punished by God! It may be
difficult to imagine, when one does not fathom the
dishonour in which so many were submerged day
and night, in the times of Jesus as they are now, in a
culture where merits were so carefully gauged.
Honour and exhilaration! Let us imagine the joyful
hearts, the dizzy heads: "What is happening to me?
I had been ever hoping for it, but how could I believe
it would come true?" Jesus not only brought comfort, cure and forgiveness. He also strewed His path
with festivities. If there was always a crowd following Him, was it not a crowd of poor people thirsting
for joyful celebrations, as very poor people always
do?

But how could they keep silent in such happy
circumstances? This is what Jesus tells those two
blind men who have groped their way behind Him,
their unseeing eyes staring into space. "Take pity on
us, Son of David!" they shouted. . . . "Do you believe

that I can heal you?" "Yes, Sir!"... "Let it happen, then, just as you believe." ...Jesus spoke sternly to them, "Don't tell this to anyone!" But they left and spread the news about Jesus all over that part of the country. (Matthew 9, 27-31)

Joy and honour again in the case of the man who stood at the entrance of the synagogue, one of his hands paralysed. He too was singled out and taken to witness. A disabled man suddenly turned into a token of the rehabilitation of the entire crowd who could not understand the prohibitions hanging over the Sabbath. These prohibitions, which may have been awkward for the rich, were virtually intolerable for the poor who had to live from day to day and for whom the Sabbath was primarily another day on which one had to survive.

Joy and honour still are given to the two blind men from Jericho. "The crowd rebuked them and told them to be quiet." Not only did they recover their sight, but they followed the Lord. Day after day, masses of people, men and women drawn from darkness to be made witnesses before the crowd and even before persons of rank, were thus restored to honour. Naturally, some of them then had to suffer painful questioning by the priests, suspicion and even ridicule. As we said before, many must also have faced uncertainty about the future. Jesus, however, spread forgiveness, rehabilitation and honour for the poorest wherever He went. And those who, after having been counted as useless or even dangerous, have partaken in this rehabilitation have never forgotten it. I wonder whether we pray enough to this Jesus who restored the poor to dignity. I also wonder whether He is given enough consideration in the services set up in our days to alleviate deprivation.

Fourth World families consider it important to be received by a head of state, or to meet high-ranking public officials with a certain degree of solemnity from time to time. Their reasons for this are different from those of others. For them, it is not a question of vanity or ambition, but of rehabilitation. A festive event took place in this perspective around the Queen of Belgium in 1982. The families were well aware that, after the occasion, everyday life would resume with its share of sorrow and anxiety. But even now they still say, "After that day, things have never been as they were before. We were restored to dignity. The Queen did not linger with the ministers; it was with us that she talked all the time."

I feel that the mass of totally impoverished families in western Europe on that day was very close to the crowds in the Gospel. Between the Queen and these families, everything could be said, even the shameful misfortune of being illiterate. In the summer heat and dust, ten thousand all too often abused people lived a day of peace and honour. Was not this atmosphere of happiness a reflection of what happened when the Son of God gathered the crowds around Him? These gatherings and rejoicings were diametrically opposed to what "bread and games" for the poor have represented through the ages. In the Gospel, around the person of Christ, we attend festivities which truly represent and programme basic change. The hardships of daily life are neither wiped out nor forgotten, but they are transformed and their meaning is reversed. "You thought you were weak and you are strong; you thought you were crushed and you are standing upright; you imagined yourself doomed and you are blessed. . . . Now that you are strong and standing up, now that odds are in your favour, you cannot stay idle, you must go strengthen your fellow men."

By restoring honour to an accursed woman and, through her, to the entire crowd of people despised by the wealthy, Jesus galvanised her. He *is* the proposed programme and His life and acts are the beginning of its application. Each gathering is a call to action but also the beginning of its implementation. Should things have been different, would very poor, sick and exhausted people have covered such distances and patiently waited for hours and days to see Christ? No doubt they did come to see and to hear. But we would underestimate them if we thought that this was the only motivation for their journeys. They certainly sensed or they knew already that, near Jesus, they would recover their dignity by receiving from Him the mission of saving their brothers. Festivals which hold no assignments of a mission are not festivals, but only entertainment. A restoration of honour which represents no call to action is a mere formality. The French Communist Party seems to have understood this better than many when it initiated the "Fête de l'Humanité." This is the yearly celebration of the party's daily newspaper. The gathering is full of entertainment, information and festive appeals to adopt the party's options. On the

1st of May, 1984, the French Confederation of Workers, for its part, organised an event of a particular nature in Paris. It was an all-at-once festive and educational fair in honour of migrant workers. Could it be that we are rediscovering honour and festivity as they were taught us two thousand years ago?

Some time ago, I attended a gathering of very poor families in the Netherlands. One lady said to me: "They used to call me Dirty Martha. This is the first time in my life that people are sitting around me and even next to me to celebrate something with me. This, I will tell everybody!" It was on the 12th of May, 1984. On that day, I dwelt in the Gospel.

CHAPTER SEVEN

The Salvation of the Poorest, a Scandal

The very poorest are healed and honoured, but they are also those who bring about offence. When I look at the world today, I am stunned by the terrible logic into which Jesus willingly entangles Himself. For people rarely tolerate that those whom they had humbled be glorified. The learned cannot admit that others, despised so far, be deemed to know more and to grasp the essentials of life.

Had a high-born man, widely recognised for his prestige, made the choice of Jesus for the poorest, perhaps his position in the world would not have been affected. Some would have thought: if this is his true conviction, there must be food for thought in it for us. Others, in the final analysis, would have forgiven him what they would have passed off as a fantasy. At worst, his milieu would have taken him for an eccentric. And eccentrics are not put to death. Christ had to be harried and crucified because He was the opposite of an eccentric. He embodied and proclaimed the deep aspirations of the poor and especially of the poorest.

Christians certainly are always ready to declare that Christ took responsibility for the hope of the very poor. But that He did so in becoming one of them remains hard to accept. Even within the Church, the very suggestion may seem an offence. "Jesus destitute, can that be true?" The question is put to me even while I write these pages. As I said before, I do not pretend to have the answer. It is not for me to prove that Jesus was born, that He lived and died as a man in utter poverty. I believe it, my eyes can see it, my ears hear it in the Gospel. I do not see Christ as one of our angry young men, leaving his familiar milieu to join the poorest. There is no single example in the Gospel presenting God's plan in this way. But it is not for me to play the part of the theologian or the philosopher. It is my task to pass on the way in which the poorest have taught me to read the Gospel and to love Jesus. I owe it to the Church to bring the very poor back to her and perhaps to help her recognise the bewildering kinship between the Son of God and the poorest around Him. It is my task to bear witness, not to present proof.

I do not know whether others could offer proof. Jesus, both Son of God and man in absolute poverty, I feel, is past human understanding. Is not the enshrinement of Godhead in the human condition the deepest of mysteries, a subject for meditation rather than for reasoning? The more we try to make the mystery yield to reason, the more it frightens us. That Jesus took as His equals men and women seemingly doing so little honour to humanity appears revolting. It seems demeaning to recognise as one's own, people literally consumed by misery to the point of being unable to show the least sign of dignity. It means self-denial and the renunciation of all the securities derived from the fact that we are human beings.

Have we any choice but to trust Christ, who had foreseen our "frights"? Relying on this word has enabled me to also take to the letter the words of Fourth World families. I have spoken before about their constant questioning: "How could they understand, those who have not had to suffer as we have?" In their eyes, Jesus could understand because He had suffered their condition. When faced with Jesus, they speak as do the men and women from certain starving hamlets in Guatemala: "We are suffering, but we shall never suffer as much as He did. We are close to Him, but even we cannot understand what He went through." These are people so exhausted by misery that no one thinks of suggesting that they participate in development projects or join a guerilla movement.

We may not always be aware of the loss we inflict upon the poor, when we let it be said that Christ has clung to at least some security by being born to another milieu, holding in fact another rank. If Jesus did not live in this world as a man in extreme poverty, then the poorest remain a marginal part of humanity

144

forever. We may then admit that Christ saved them *also*, salvation being extended to them through the better-off. But we shall not acknowledge that Christ saved them *first* and saved humanity through them. Thus we perpetuate as it were a last and final spoliation. For the very poor would then be sub-human creatures whom the Son of God could pity but whose identity He could not make His own. We would assume grievous responsibility indeed. By the very way in which He came into the world, Christ established priorities and even preferences. Do we make sure not to overturn these? In order to break down our social hierarchies, did Jesus place Himself on one of the lower rungs of the social scale? Or did He, from birth, stay at the very foot of the ladder, in the midst of this part of humanity considered guilty because it frightened the better-off?

We are faced with this question again by the healing of the man born blind. (John 9, 1-41) The disciples express all the bewilderment we still feel today in our public institutions, at Caritas or the Salvation Army. The man at the entrance of the synagogue was not only stricken with blindness, he was also a beggar. Not all blind people in Jesus' days were equally deprived. "And the neighbours, who had grown accustomed to seeing him beg, would ask, 'Is he not the one who used to sit there begging? Rabbi, whose sins caused him to be born blind? Were they his parents' or his own?'" Incomprehensible as it may seem, people still ask the very same question today. Generally speaking, they know much more about eye diseases. But when it comes to children in extreme poverty, nothing seems to have changed.

Do we not witness unending discussions about whether very poor children come into the world already tainted or whether their environment gradually leads them to failure in school, to juvenile delinquency and chronic unemployment before they have ever held a job? This was the situation of young people in very poor housing areas, long before general economic recession struck other social strata. So often, in endless meetings involving various ministries, I heard these discussions on the roots of evil. I felt I was listening to the disciples: "But then, whose fault is it? Why is he tainted, what is the original cause? Does it lie with the parents or with the children?", the question apparently implying that the cause could not lie with us. These people were too different from us, they existed apart from us, in spite of us, in no way *because* of us.

Some will object that I take physical disease for extreme poverty. In a way, I do. Deep poverty and physical disability often overlap, one evil intensifying the other and the two contributing together to the destruction of human beings. It is therefore difficult to know what people think about either one. Our purpose is not to study people's attitudes toward disability or extreme poverty. Our purpose is to contemplate the Lord among the poorest. It is with them who are afflicted by so many infirmities that Christ begins to liberate the poor, the wealthy and all people. Are we in communion with Him in anguish, as we see Him stride toward the scandal that is bound to befall Him because of the people He chooses to befriend? Walking with Jesus through the Gospel, we notice that those He prefers frighten the others or at least receive little respect. They are considered pernicious, sinful, or, at least, contemptible. The crowd, which unceasingly carries along its sick and miserable, refers us to present-day realities. We know a similar crowd, expressing itself and being discussed by others, now as in Jesus' time. Today's crowd is also poor and its poverty can still lead to that extreme where a new-born child is laid down on scraps of cardboard in midwinter. And this child is also considered guilty. To this, we must bear witness. No sociological study, however interesting, can contribute as much as does our communion with the poorest today, our ears filled with their voices, our eyes beholding their faces, their pain and their inordinate hopes enshrined in our hearts.

Such constant meditation necessarily brings us nearer to all humanity, rich and poor alike. We get a fairer view of humanity, which is all too often judged for its failing generosity, rather than pitied for its genuine and often overwhelming anxiety in the face of misery linked with disease and rendering repulsive fellow people most in need of love. For this humanity so deeply confused ("Rabbi, who was it who sinned?"), God alone would restore the truth about man that man himself had obscured. But at what cost?

At one side, we see the crowd: "You are the Son of David. . .", "He is the prophet Jesus of Nazareth in Galilee." On the other side stand the Pharisees, the priests whom we perhaps typecast too often as heartless, wealthy people always ready to set traps for the poor. Had they been no better than that, would Christ have spent so many hours discussing things with them? They were not only responsible for the people; many must also have been genuinely concerned for them. And Jesus, in debating with them, took them seriously, even as they talked to Him in real earnest themselves. Their discussions have the same quality of truth as all that occurs in Jesus' life. The issue constantly debated is the truth about God and His justice and, consequently, about the place of the small and the humble in His love. With anything less at stake, would antagonism have become so sharp? All my life's experience in the depths of poverty inclines me to believe that Jesus' preference for the poorest was the real source of the scandal gradually built up around His person.

Let us return to the synagogue where a heated debate ends up in confusing battle and even intrigue around a totally deprived and vulnerable man. Born blind and without parents or friends able to feed him, he is forced to wait for those around him to set food out for him. He has, of course, no education and knows of the world only that which he can sense by touching. Of the seasons, he feels the succession in his body; of the time that passes, he knows only the endlessness, but not what gives it rhythm and significance. He does not see what changes and evolves in things and people. Born blind, almost stillborn, he is talked *about*, never spoken *to*. Is he innocent or a sinner? He has no means to answer the question himself. Had he opened his mouth, his words would no doubt have been muddled as are the words of so many who, deprived of education and respect, feel themselves unjustly accused. I remember a father who always had great difficulty in sticking to a consistent argument. One day, he said to me, "Look at me. Everybody always takes me for a nitwit. In the end, all I can do is drop to all fours and bark. They say I am a bad father to my kids and I don't know how to argue with them."

The blind man, guilty or innocent? On the occurrence of his healing, we find a curious annotation in the footnotes of the "Traduction Oecumenique" of the Bible. Commentaries remark that "Jesus sidesteps prevailing theories without proposing a new one. He notes the infirmity as a fact and does what is needed to ensure to this man full physical ability. At the same time, He offers him the sign which will allow him to accede to 'genuine light'." Should not the commentary go further? When Christ heals the disabled with the "leitmotif": "Your faith has saved you," some will hasten to add that He first of all confirms God's mercy for the sinners. Based on what justification do they say so? Relying on what happened between Jesus and Satan, we would rather tend to say that God extended His mercy, first of all to the poor and the powerless, and through them to *all* people. In the face of the man born blind, no more than on any other occasion, Jesus brushes aside a current theory without taking the pains to propose a new answer. What could induce us to impute such triviality to Jesus, especially with regard to the disciples who will still have to face so many difficulties in answering the world's questions in His name?

The words and deeds exchanged between Jesus and the very poorest are always unique, perfectly attuned to each personality, and yet a symbol for all.

They clearly challenge and overturn an overall situation created around them by others, often in the name of God. For it is in the name of God that a blind man must remain on the outskirts of the Temple, prohibited from entering the inner precincts freely, as do the healthy. The overall condition of the poor, the place to be occupied by the sick and disabled in the community as in the Temple, which reduced all the invalids among the poor to sheer misery—all this was regulated in the name of God. Jesus at all times takes a stand, overturns a rule, restoring not only honour to one person, but justice to all. At every turn, He proclaims the freedom of all God's children, be they ever so poor. He proclaims the truth, now publicly, speaking out, now intimately, before only the disciples. But the message is always unequivocal: God loves us and the destiny of our fellow men and women is as essential to us as our own future. This is the permanent proclamation in the name of the Father, never concealed nor watered down, which is steadily leading the Lord into the scandal prepared for Him. Each time He compromises Himself with the most wretched, we see Him more certainly doomed to His ignominious death.

On this particular day, Jesus, upon leaving the Temple, does not avoid the essential issue. His answer is clear: the question about guilt is not as you put it; the real question lies elsewhere. God knows no scapegoats. If you are faced with a cripple submerged in misery, remember that he is there to instruct you "so that the works of God become manifest" in that person. Personally, I do not know many more beautiful words in the Gospel. Go to the poorest without delay, draw close around them, be silent before them and love them, for in them the works of God become manifest. From them, you will learn to cooperate in these works, renouncing all others. Go reveal to them their role in God's plan. To learn about their mission is the very first of their human rights. You, who imagine yourself better versed in these matters, know that they will understand more easily than you.

All this I discover in the words of Jesus, who freed the poorest as none other ever has or will. Or rather, Fourth World families make me read His words this way, day by day. Of all that the Gospel teaches them, this privileged participation in God's works is most accessible and familiar to them. In all my contacts, I bow to the same intimacy between God and the most wretched among His children. "We suffer, and therefore we are with our Lord," said the mother of a family in total deprivation in a Brazilian village. It had taken her some time to grasp the ideas developed with the villagers on stocking corn and small-scale irrigation. These plans were certainly of interest to her. But to both her neighbours and herself, participating in the works of God had quite a different significance.

Jesus puts questions on sin, on the blessed, on those who will precede others in their proper place and perspective. We saw the example of the Samaritan woman. The Sermon on the Mount and the Lord's teaching on the Last Judgment will shed further light. The issue will always be the works of God which must become manifest in the most downcast among people. "While it is still day, we must labour in the works of He who sent me," said Jesus, while suiting the action to the word and restoring to the beggar both his eyesight and human dignity. An awe-inspiring gesture! Even as God made the human race, His Son took earth between His fingers to recreate a low-born man and make him new and unique forever.

The healed man will be amazed by what happens to him, being questioned as he is after having bathed his eyes at Siloé. "Who are you? Who has restored your sight?" There he stands before the Pharisees: "So this happened to you on the day of the Sabbath? And you dare pretend that the healer is, moreover, a prophet?" Here come the parents, obviously poor themselves. "Watch your words now: is this really your son who was blind? Then you had better explain how it is that he can see now!" This scene reminds me of another I recently witnessed in a slum area: "So, your son who does not earn a penny and has never held a job suddenly possesses a motorbike! And you pretend that it was given to him, but you don't even know by whom?" No wonder the parents, cautious as all people are in front of those who have power, stick to a single response, "I know nothing about it, I saw nothing. . . ."

There is something pathetic and humiliating for us all about this man who is ill-treated when he should have inspired general rejoicing. The Pharisees summon him once more, gradually turning his cure into sheer misfortune! "What exactly did He do to you? How did He open your eyes?" This man, suddenly released among the seeing, looks at the contorted faces around him. None would think of praising this day of miraculous recovery. How did he bear it all? "I told you already, but you did not listen." Half ironically, half naïvely, he even adds, "Are you not willing to become His disciples?" Let us listen carefully to his extraordinary answer to those who advise him to mistrust Jesus.

> "As for that fellow,
> we do not even know where He comes from."
> The man answered,
> "What a strange thing that is!
> You do not know where He comes from,
> but He cured me of my blindness!
> We know that God does not listen to sinners;
> He does listen to people who respect Him
> and do His will.
> Since the beginning of the world,
> nobody has ever heard
> of anyone giving sight to a blind person.
> Unless this man came from God,
> He would not be able to do a thing."

(John 9, 24-35)

No intellectual, be he priest, scribe or Pharisee, would have answered this way. Obviously this man was only echoing what he had been told over all those years of sitting on the Temple steps: "There is no cure for you. There are reasons for your affliction. You must take it in patience. For God to answer your prayers, you should have been more pious." It is his turn to cast these words in the faces of those who spoke them while leaving him to his fate as a beggar.

"Only God can and will do what you yourselves deemed impossible and even unfitting." The man, now healed, fills our ears with years and years of pent-up suffering and humiliation at last put into words. We also note that he brushes aside all theoretical debate. "So much for your theories," is the gist of what he says. "I know but one thing, namely that I was blind, and now I can see." A long time ago, I heard a man who had once lived in a trailer speak that way. He was totally impoverished and had been evicted from his apartment with his wife and children. Yet, he stubbornly refused to return to life in a fairly broken-down trailer offered by local authorities. Public officials in the Town Hall took great pains to argue with him, explaining that, after all, he was accustomed to living in a trailer. He would feel at home there and have no more problems. Some friends miraculously found him an old forester's cabin in good repair. Here is what he said to the people at the Town Hall who showed irritation at the solution: "I know but one thing. I had a roof no longer and now I have one." And he added these unforgettable words, "You are the ones who say that I am unable to live in a house because I was once a traveller, but you are not God the Father!"

In the meantime, there we are, the boundless joy of the man healed of blindness not only turned to ridicule, but giving rise to indignation and resentment. It is hard to believe, yet John writes it out in full. While this man was barely recovering from endless years in pain, "the Pharisees started insulting him." This is not the first time, nor will it be the

154

last. Throughout the Gospel, the joy of the poor is frequently turned into a scandal. This represents a humiliating reality for all of us. Did the Saviour really have to go through all this, did the very poor so constantly have to suffer with Him in order to save us? The participation of the poorest in the world's salvation, even in Jesus' own days, their inability to avoid bringing scandal, should be the focus of our meditation and prayer. Why is it that the honours and joy bestowed upon them seem unbearable to those around them ?

I am well aware that this question recurs again and again throughout these pages, even as it recurs in my daily life. Why all these grudges against them, why so much harassment inflicted upon them? Why did we meet with such fierce opposition ourselves when we declared that, for the poorest among families, harmonious housing, beautiful kindergartens, and People's Universities fitted out in good taste were in order? How often were we made to understand that "concrete walls are what these people need. No reason to invite vandalism. Let's make sure not to plan anything fancy that would make them feel out of place."

Let us suppose that the blind man had been the son of a Pharisee or the man with the paralysed hand or the blind, deaf and possessed man (Matthew 12, 9-14 and 22-24) the sons of a doctor of law. We need not even pose this question for the cripple at the pool of Bethesda. Had he been higher born, he would not have spent thirty-eight years waiting there. Let us surmise however that many of these healings could have happened among the better-off. Can we reasonably believe that they would then have sparked off all these questions about the Sabbath, Jesus' authority, or the source of His powers? We are told that the scrupulous insistence of the Pharisees on the observance of the Sabbath was by no means unusual. Indeed, in order to safeguard the Jewish religion and faith against all impurity, they had barricaded them in a scaffolding of rules and regulations. But everyone knows, and the Pharisees best of all, that the more rules there are, the easier one rule can serve to annul another. Those who possess knowledge have profited from this since the world has existed. Rules bind those who are held in ignorance. Would they have been quoted against Jesus if, instead of healing paupers, He had laid His hands on the more well-to-do? He did so occasionally, without provoking outcries, it seems. Would He then have been considered to be doing the works of Beëlzebub, another bogeyman used to frighten off the crowds?

We have all the more difficulty in believing it as we must witness the continuous contempt for the joy of the humble. They must consider themselves lucky if they are allowed to leave in silence, without rejoicing or praise, but at least unmolested.

Then He said to the man with
the paralysed hand,
"Stretch out your hand."
He stretched it out, and it became well again,
just like the other one.
Then the Pharisees left
and made plans to kill Jesus.
(Matthew 12, 13-14)

156

In this case, Jesus and His companions were at least able to leave quietly. But what antagonism against the poorest must have filled the hearts of the Pharisees who, when seeing a possessed, blind or mute beggar healed of such a burden of woe, would hasten to shout to the crowd: "Beware that you do not rejoice! What happens to you is no blessing, but a curse. It is Beëlzebub working among you!" Did they not know how much their people suffered? Must they stifle all consolation and gladness this way? Was it really necessary to penalise not only the healing of one poor man, but *all* the healings achieved in Gennesaret, on the riverbank, in the mountains, and all over?

Unless we want to ascribe a truly inhuman wickedness to the Pharisees, we are bound to think of the fear that invades them. We have already spoken of this deep-seated fear, which is not so much a real worry about the orthodoxy of a people's faith as fright of men and women disfigured by misery. To make these poverty-stricken people throng the road and rejoice meant not only that the established order was overthrown, but that all order ever invented by people was annulled. I said before that the divinity of Jesus was brought home to me by His choice of the most rejected. This choice scandalised the entire Jewish community, and even the poor who were part of it. Let us meditate once more on the staggering story of the healing at the pool of Bethesda.

After this,
Jesus went to Jerusalem for a religious festival.
Near the Sheep Gate in Jerusalem,

157

there is a pool with five porches;
in Hebrew, it is called Bethesda.
A large crowd of sick people
were lying on the porches—
the blind, the lame and the paralysed.
A man was there who had been ill
for thirty-eight years.
Jesus saw him lying there,
and He knew that the man had been ill
for such a long time;
So He asked him, "Do you want to get well?"
The sick man answered,
"Sir, I have no one here
to put me in the pool
when the water is stirred up;
while I am trying to get in,
somebody else gets there first."
Jesus said to him,
"Get up, pick up your mat and walk."
Immediately, the man got well;
he picked up his mat and started walking.
The day this happened was a Sabbath,
so the Jewish authorities
told the man who had been healed,
"This is the Sabbath,
and it is against our law for you
to carry your mat."
He answered,
"The man who made me well told me,
to pick up my mat and walk."
They asked him,
"Who is the man who told you to do this?"
But the man who had been healed

did not know who Jesus was,
for there was a crowd in that place
and Jesus had slipped away.
Afterwards Jesus found him in the Temple and
said,
"Listen, you are well now,
So stop sinning or something worse may
happen to you."
Then the man left and told the Jewish
authorities
that it was Jesus who had healed him.
So, they began to persecute Jesus
because He had done this healing
on a Sabbath.
Jesus answered them,
"My Father is always working,
and I too must work."
This saying made the Jewish authorities
all the more determined to kill Him;
not only had He broken the Sabbath law,
but He had said that God was His own Father
and in this way, had made Himself equal with
God.

(John 5, 1-18)

We have before our eyes the five porches where an unspeakable mass of the disabled has taken shelter in constant jostling. It is hard to imagine their pitiful state and their callousness among one another. They each want their places and the stronger will secure the best ones. Endless waiting, sudden warnings—"the water begins to stir"—and sad disappointment keep nerves on edge. "It's because of

159

you that I did not get to the pool, you got in my way. . . ." Bethesda is a place of untold misery, tension, and degradation. Indeed, the world rarely leaves the very poor a chance to safeguard outward signs of dignity. "They look at us as if we had the plague," people in hard-core poverty areas often say. What then must have been the lot of the unshapely mass of crippled and lame under the colonnades of Bethesda?

Intent on penetrating ever more deeply into human misery, Jesus has made His way to Jerusalem. Here, the crowd of the miserable, the maimed and the beggars is beyond description. Jerusalem, like all sacred cities, all sites of cathedrals and pilgrimages throughout the ages, attracted them. Cities like these are, as it were, a last refuge, a last chance to receive alms. Such situations have always ended up by calling forth regulations to stay the overflow of the miserable and limit the nuisance they cause. Hearts and customs gradually harden against them. The fact that some mutilated themselves or feigned being mutilated obviously did not enhance communication or brotherly feelings.

At the pool of Bethesda, Jesus in a way has reached the end of the road laid out since the temptation and even since Bethlehem. And in the midst of the unshapely mass, He has found the most wretched of all. He finds the paralytic friend lost in the crowd of disabled and yet chosen from among them all, since thirty-eight years of suffering and neglect have driven him to desperation and broken his spirit. When the Lord asks him, "Do you want to get well?", he dares not even reply, "Yes, I do." He says only what say all the forsaken who know there is no escape for them: "Sir, I have no one. . . ."

"I have no one. . . ." How often I have heard this reply to my awkward questioning: "Could not your family take in the children for a few weeks, just long enough to avoid their being taken into foster care?" . . . "Could not someone take your defence in court, since you are innocent?" . . . "Father, I have no one. . ." "Father, look at my roof which is coming down, I have no one. . ." "Father, I don't dare think of the money I owe, I have no one." I can still hear the father of one family speaking that way on a winter's night. He was sitting there in his makeshift shelter, surrounded by his children, shivering because there was no wood or coal to make a fire. "I asked the people at the parish. They told me to go to the social worker. But she said there was nothing she could do. She was not supposed to provide heating." Every time I face these families with no one to turn to and locked up in their solitude, I face the situation of the paralytic in Bethesda.

When one has reached the bottom of misery, even people officially designated to offer assistance (as in the case of public services) will ultimately forsake one. They get tired of being harassed by requests, of making efforts to no avail. They realise that their piecemeal help can in no way cure the evil of a vicious cycle of deprivations. Patching is no use; what is needed is entirely new cloth. This discouragement is further entrenched by the hesitations, fears and sudden withdrawals of the families themselves, by the aggressive attitudes which for no apparent reason take the place of their former trust.

161

However sincere the initial goodwill of those who were supposed to help, disappointment sets in sooner or later. I still see one man, furiously chasing a social worker down the stairs, because she had made a remark which, in his edginess, he had taken for an insult. She had meant well, but he was the unemployed head of a family, driven out of his wits by anxiety.

While I write these pages, it is snowing over Paris. I know families here who live in dilapidated housing where water and electricity have been cut off. Completely discouraged, all social services have given up and even the most basic commodities have been withdrawn by an unseeing hand, as if to seal an ultimate abandonment. Do we realise what it means to have the water cut off in a family with small children living on the fifth floor of a decrepit building in the Paris area? Do we know what it represents to be deprived of all means of doing the laundry, bathing, cooking and doing the dishes? Can we imagine how it feels to see oneself and one's family so degraded in one of these low-rent housing projects falling into ruins with its dilapidated frontage and its interior in constant overall disrepair?

Such a family, to be sure, will turn to a slightly better-off neighbour, but that household is already helping many others. In an extremely poor housing area, it is not easy to figure among those who still have something to share because the father has a job. I have seen women driven to charging for their water, just to stop the endless procession of pails, the dirty footsteps in their doorway, the water sloshing to the floor. Not to speak of the shameful procession of pails which must replace the water closet.

In the evenings, left without light, without electricity to warm the only hot plate, parents and children sit alone in the dark, listening to their neighbours who still live normally, their apartments alight and the radio or television at full-blast. What can they talk about? There is nothing left to say, except to cast blame, "You could have been more careful. . . . You could have made an effort. . . ." Christ said, "Those who love the truth live in the light, they seek the light." I sometimes wonder what it actually means to us to accept that families already much deprived must live without electricity. To knock on a door at night and find a family in the dark has always reminded me of the total neglect inflicted on the paralytic under the colonnade at the pool of Bethesda.

Extreme poverty creates a vacuum around people, and the very poor share Christ's solitude in the garden of Gethsemene. There, Jesus will experience the epitome of all the loneliness come over Him, having been misunderstood and abandoned by all. On the cross, He will for a last time cry out this pain, "My God, my God, why have You forsaken me?" For when all have forsaken one, is it not God Himself who has deserted one? On His way to this final solitude, Christ could not have failed to recognise and single out amongst all others the paralytic who had no one to help him. This man will utter to Him the complaint that will soon be His own: "I am totally abandoned." And this very lamentation will echo through the ages to reach our own ears. "Father, my husband has turned me out in the middle of the night, please open the door. Here I am with my children and no one to turn to." Even as the blind man, whom I found tied to a tree outside a village in the bush, had no one to turn to. His wife and children beside him had no land to till. Nor had this sick widow anyone to turn to, with her five children in a Brazilian shanty atop a hill, far beyond reach of the water supply system. "Ah, Dios!... If God existed, would He leave me like this?" she asked me. "If God existed," another woman said, "do you think that my little boy would be beaten up at school because he comes from a slum or because they say he stinks?" "If God exists,..." said a young father in the Netherlands, "the tragedy is that He exists and does not think of us."

The complaint of the paralytic is the complaint of Jesus and of the very poor of all times. It is hard to imagine his state of mind when being told to walk and feeling his legs respond for the first time. To walk, but where to? To the Temple, of course, to give thanks to God. Engrossed as he was in his miraculous happiness, what must he have thought of those people of influence starting to pick on him instead of rejoicing with him? He was the first to understand Jesus telling him, "Now that you are cured, be sure to sin no more, so that nothing worse may happen to you." Thirty-eight years of helplessness, begging and neglect are not forgotten overnight. From now on, this man is free and therefore responsible for his deeds. Will he be able to stand upright, to live among men in dignity? Jesus' warning is to the point. But what to think of these Temple officials who ignore his joy and pettily admonish him for carrying his mat on the day of the Sabbath? What must he have thought of these people of distinction who created so strange an atmosphere around such a marvellous event? Our paralytic friend, beloved of the Lord, have you ever known that because of you the stranglehold of public outrage was going to tighten around the Saviour of humanity?

CHAPTER EIGHT

The Penitent Thief,
A Companion for Eternity

Two more people wait for us in the Gospel, publicly loaded with the blame of their entire community: he whom we call the penitent thief and Mary Magdalene. Two more persons, each conveying a unique message from our Lord and to whom I frequently return. Were they among the poorest all their lives? Possibly, but more importantly: their existence led them to a state of extreme contempt. That is how Jesus finds them and to each of them He is going to make a promise which will become a promise forever. His meeting with them represents as it were a pinnacle, the ultimate confirmation of His life. Through them we shall learn once again that to be rejected on earth can be the path to total faith in God.

Let us draw near to Calvary where three crosses stand out against the sky.

When they came to the place
called "The Skull,"
they crucified Jesus there, and the two criminals,
one on His right and the other on His left.
Jesus said, "Forgive them, Father!
For they know not what they do."
They divided His clothes among themselves
by throwing dice.
The people stood there watching
while the Jewish leaders jeered at Him:
"He saved others; let Him save Himself
if He is the Messiah whom God has chosen!"
The soldiers also mocked Him: they came up to Him
and offered Him cheap wine, and said,
"Save yourself, if you are the king of the Jews!"
Above Him were written these words:
"This is the king of the Jews."
One of the criminals hanging there
hurled insults at Him:
"Aren't you the Messiah? Save yourself and us!"
The other one, however, rebuked him, saying,
"Don't you fear God?
You received the same sentence as He did.
Ours, however, is only right
because we are getting
what we deserve for what we did;
but He has done no wrong."
And he said to Jesus, "Remember me, Jesus,
when you come as King!"
Jesus said to him, "I promise you

167

that today you will be in Paradise with me."

(Luke 23, 33-43)

Let us try to imagine the background of this man whom Christianity took to calling the penitent thief, perhaps without always realising the term's deep significance. He comes from a milieu in and around Jerusalem where huddle ruffians, cripples, thieves, men and women rightly or wrongly suspected of every vice, a milieu where delinquency and misery mingle. More directly, the penitent thief comes from prison and we know what must have been prison life among a people bled dry by the Roman oppression, by tax-collectors and priests. Where people are poor, prisons are places where poor people guard even poorer fellow men and women. The prisoners are hardly fed and are often prey to the frustration, vengeance and even sadism of their jailers. Torture finds a natural home in such confinement, as it always does when chained and helpless prisoners are abandoned to the mercy of jailers whose own lives are harsh. If we in the rich countries had not forgotten this, would we feel perhaps that we share responsibility for torture in famine and disease-ridden parts of the world?

We now see this man nailed to the cross, a horrifying sight with his already shattered body and disfigured face. But we also imagine what goes on in his heart and mind: all the brutality he has suffered, all the violence he has inflicted himself. They have modelled his inner self and his language. No doubt he has heard about Jesus. Did he perhaps see Him or even follow Him one day? Did Jesus' existence light a flicker of hope in his heart, as it did for so many other poor and wretched people? In any case, he recognises the Son of God on the Cross. At that moment all his doubts vanish. His hope is now boundless.

About himself, he says first of all that his punishment is just. How often I have heard men and women say this, agreeing to pay for acts which I considered due to society's failings, rather than their own. "I have stolen, I got caught, and now I go to jail. That's only normal." I remember my friend Richard, whose life had been one ceaseless series of failures and humiliations. After fighting with the police in a pub at Ivry he said to those who arrested him, "I punched them, I played the fool, I'll come with you now, it's only normal." Among the very poorest, I have continually found this need to make amends, to pay as it were for a whole life of blundering, of uncontrolled anger and thoughtless violence. The profound need for forgiveness makes them accept the punishment as does the penitent thief. "It's only normal...." Was it normal too for the hardened ruffian to recognise immediately that the man on the cross beside him had done no wrong? I think so, particularly if the thief himself was a victim of extreme poverty. At all events, we witness the most deeply moving scene of mutual recognition. "Remember me, Jesus, when You come into Your Kingdom." ... "Today you will be in Paradise with me." In this last encounter, Jesus is going to sum up His entire teaching about God's love.

The thief does not ask forgiveness, for he is already

paying for his deeds. His only request is the one we hear again and again from the very poor who realise they are incapable of pleading their case themselves: "Remember me...," "Speak for me, plead for me, you who know the right people and what to say...." Is this not the age-old desperate appeal of the wretched, seeking a defender to recommend them to those who judge and decide? "You, who know people, put in a word for me to the welfare officer, the trade union representative, the local councillor, the boss." They dare not go for themselves, convinced as they are that they can neither explain nor defend their case. They feel undeserving, they fear that no one will believe them. Someone else will carry more weight, have a better chance to succeed.

In His last face to face encounter, Jesus hears this standing cry once more and His reply is immediate. He will not say that the thief is innocent. He only replies, "If the community rejects you, if society casts you out, you still remain one of God's children." Indeed, how could there be a final and lasting break between human beings and the Father? A human community can destroy one of its members, delete him from its memory. For God, such a death penalty cannot exist. Through His life and death, Christ cancels all exclusion. "I return to the Father, my hands and feet pierced; I shall enter Paradise as the Crucified One for eternity, and you are my chosen companion. They who accompanied me in life shall also be my companions in the Kingdom."

Surely these words of Jesus were a final confirmation, proclaimed from the Cross, that God can reject none of His children, nor deny affiliation to even the least of them. People may refuse to recognise a brother or sister, but God can withdraw from none the right to come back to Him. Whatever their sins or prostration, all remain His children.

Jesus takes the penitent thief with Him to the Kingdom as a witness to that new alliance which, in order to encompass all, must begin with the most excluded of all. Never again will anyone suffer rejection in this world without someone standing witness before the Father that he will be welcomed and loved. Jesus returns to His Father having taken upon Himself all the misery, all the suffering of humanity. Whatever may be the existence of this mother scavenging in trash cans or resorting to prostitution to feed her children, whoever may be this man insulting his neighbour or throwing out his son, whatever may become of this child shoplifting in a supermarket, all are saved, for all eternity. The Son of God is sitting at His right hand, marked by the nails which sealed His death. And at His side we see the penitent thief, warranting the alliance which binds God to the most miserable among them.

The penitent thief, as we said, does not ask forgiveness. The time for that has past, since his death is also his purification. He has now entered the realm of mercy. So many people thus reach death, as the final outcome of an uninterrupted sequence of misery and suffering. Apparently they can no longer be good nor pardoned, swept away as they are in the grip of violence, fear and cowardice. I feel this must have been the state of mind of the penitent thief, in prison and right up to his crucifixion. His life and death must have been such an ordeal that Jesus could say, "It is all over now, your sins are remitted. God will ask no more of you. Today you will be in Paradise."

I have seen so many people haunted night and day by pain, shame and the feeling of being totally abandoned. I cannot imagine their entry in the Kingdom otherwise. How indeed could God heap additional suffering, inflict further penitence on those whom the world has already so severely punished? It would be contrary to His divine mercy, contrary to the promise given by His Son, "You have recognised me, I have recognised you, you will be my companion for all eternity."

This alliance I feel will also extend to the supposedly unrepentant thief, as it will to all humanity. Would not the mystery of God, who can admit no break with humanity, hold for all? On the cross with the penitent thief Christ redefines for one last time the terms of the contract: the Eucharist will be the permanent token of the Crucified before His Father, whom He perfectly obeys in all things. "Just as you see me now, just as I see you, we shall both be in Paradise." The penitent thief will be the only witness in the Gospel to receive such a promise. But in so stating His refusal of exclusion, does Christ not say that from now on all will be drawn to the Kingdom, rich and poor, penitent and unrepentant thieves alike?

Through the penitent thief, Jesus Christ seems to want to make us understand something vital about the share to be paid. There is no fixed price for entry into the Kingdom. Each person retains a share of communion with human suffering. The share retained by the poor is more than their hands can hold. They do not enter Paradise as special favourites to whom the Father has granted a preference. They are first to enter because they have stocked up a greater share of suffering than anyone else. But all God's children have their place waiting and who amongst them will not sooner or later have his part in the sufferings, the contempt, failure, and humiliation of the others? This part, each of us may turn to account with God as a token of our affiliation to Him.

Is not this the explanation of Christ's words, "There are many rooms in my Father's house"? This way we can understand the exaltation of the humble, the humiliation of the mighty. We can be quite sure that there are no grades of happiness, no special merits to be sought in Paradise. The poor at least do not think so. Nor is this the vision given by Jesus of a Kingdom where all will be one, the poor having received the good tidings. But Jesus left us ground for constant meditation and questioning about those who precede us into the Kingdom, about the road to choose and the share to acquire, if we want to follow them.

Christ not only died as a villain, He suffered His passion in the company of villains. I remember how I celebrated the Eucharist at the Camp of the Homeless in Noisy-le-Grand, as I remember so many other holy masses celebrated in areas of extreme poverty, broken-down housing and desolation. Around me in the chapel were men considered "good-for-nothing" and undesirable, some of them quarrelling among themselves, some not entirely sober. The women were often nervous and on edge, their minds elsewhere, "What meal can I serve after the funeral?" "What shall I give to the children this Christmas Eve?" Yet I knew they were all in search of hope and forgiveness. Among them, it seemed to me, the Eucharist fully achieved its purpose. I remember a man who accidently killed his five-year-old daughter. He had slapped her and, as she fell, her head had struck a corner of the stove. She died on the spot. The distraught parents dug her a grave in the earthen floor of their hovel, under their own bed. For five years they slept over their little girl's body and the mother gradually went mad. They said that the child had gone to live with an aunt. In any case, no one really kept track of the numbers of children among these families huddled together at the gateways of Paris. Yet, in the end, they were denounced by a neighbour. The father was condemned to death, his sentence subsequently commuted to life imprisonment. I think of him on Good Friday when we are brought face to face with the penitent thief. This story is by no means exceptional. There is so much more despair than we imagine, there are so many penitent thieves in the abyss at the foot of our social scale.

The penitent thief himself was not an exceptional criminal, singled out for the occasion. It is my deep conviction—let me say this again—that the birth and death of Jesus represented no special events created for the sake of demonstration. I feel they were part and parcel of a perfectly unified existence. They also represented the everyday realities of a society that was itself perfectly coherent in its acts and in the situations it created for its members. A society where Jesus was born in a condition of dire need, where later on He had nowhere to lay His head at night in dignity and security, and where He was destined to die outside the city walls, as the outcast He had been from the beginning.

The presence of the penitent thief at the hour of His death, the promise Jesus made that he would enter Paradise, confirm the oneness of His life, the coherence of His plan and His utter integrity. Without that presence, without His promise, would the poor ever have been set free?

CHAPTER NINE

Mary Magdalene,
the Church's First Steps

Early on Sunday morning, while it was still dark,
Mary Magdalene went to the tomb
and saw that the stone had been taken away
from the entrance.
She went running to Simon Peter and the other
*   disciple,*
whom Jesus loved, and told them,
"They have taken the Lord from the tomb
and we don't know where they have put Him!"
Then Peter and the other disciple went to the tomb.
The two of them were running,
but the other disciple ran faster than Peter
and reached the tomb first.
He bent over and saw the linen wrappings,

but he did not go in.
Behind him came Simon Peter,
and he went straight into the tomb.
He saw the linen wrappings lying there
and the cloth which had been round Jesus' head.
It was not lying with the linen wrappings
but was rolled up by itself. Then the other disciple,
who had reached the tomb first,
also went in; he saw and believed.
(They still did not understand the scripture
which said that He must rise from death.)
Then the disciples went back home.
Mary stood crying outside the tomb.
While she was still crying, she bent over
and looked in the tomb and saw two angels there
*   dressed in white,*
sitting where the body of Jesus had been,
one at the head and the other at the feet.
"Woman, why are you crying?" they asked her.
She answered, "They have taken my Lord away,
and I do not know where they have put Him!"
Then she turned round
and saw Jesus standing there;
but she did not know that it was Jesus.
"Woman, why are you crying?" Jesus asked her.
"Who is it that you are looking for?"
She thought He was the gardener,
so she said to Him,
"If you took Him away, sir,
tell me where you have put Him
and I will go and get Him."
Jesus said to her, "Mary!"
She turned towards Him and said out in Hebrew,

"Rabboni!", which means Teacher.
"Do not hold on to me," Jesus told her,
"because I have not yet gone back up to the Father.
But go to my brothers and tell them
that I am returning to Him who is my Father
and their Father,
my God and their God."
So Mary Magdalene went and told the disciples
that she had seen the Lord
and related to them what He had told her.

(John 20, 1-18)

Was Mary Magdalene, the first to recognise Christ, alone or with other women? The main point is that she was there, the first witness, preceding even the disciples. And the risen Christ was still the same Jesus, choosing a human being He had drawn from darkness, healed, pardoned and saved, to be the messenger of crucial news. He chose no disciple, not even Peter or John, but a woman from the fringe of society where were relegated the sinners alleged to call down curses. A world of blind and possessed, of adulterous women and beggars, of poor people branded impure, a world of sin, exclusion and misery; it is here that the risen Christ has chosen His first messenger.

For who was Mary of Magdala? According to Mark, Jesus had driven seven devils from her. Can we picture the situation of a possessed woman in ancient Galilee? Who looked after her, who fed her? Did someone leave a bowl of food for her, somewhere, at a distance to avoid contamination?

178

Somewhere in the heart of Africa, south of the Sahara, at the end of an impassable trail, in a hamlet of some ten huts, the straw shelter of an epileptic woman has caught fire. Half her body has been burnt by the flames. The neighbours have laid her on a bed of ashes to absorb her urine. No one has gone to warn the missionaries or the head of the district infirmary a few miles away. Brother Jacques Thiébaud, a Capuchin missionary touring the bush, has found the woman. They have exchanged a few words. Then, before a handful of peasants, women and frightened children, Brother Jacques, having seen to some essential first aid, baptises her, administers holy communion and confirms her. All the villagers dressed in rags, as are most people along this terrible trail, are not able to understand what went on. But all have witnessed the peace and tenderness brought to that woman. All have seen her honour restored to her: "Your soul is not possessed by evil spirits, you are saved...." And through her, the entire hamlet knows it has recovered its dignity.

Haunted as they were by the fear of demons, the villagers were ready to let one among them perish, a defenceless injured woman, inevitably possessed by evil forces. By re-establishing the truth about humanity ("You are the child of God, loved and saved by Him"), Brother Jacques not only prepared the epileptic woman for the approaching feast of the Resurrection. By his act of liberation he restored the whole hamlet to a new order. "Will you look after her now?" he asked, as he took leave. "We will," promised the peasants.

In fact, what Brother Jacques did, what he and his

whole mission do from day to day in that forsaken region in the heart of Africa is no more than to follow the example of Jesus. They repeat the acts of Christ who healed the sick brought to Him by the crowds, those He knew would never lift up their heads nor think of rebuilding the world unless they heard these words, "Go in peace, God loves you, you are saved." Only then can other actions follow and can people consumed by malnutrition and fear concern themselves with better crops, education or health care. But among the Christians of Europe, who but the mission remembers how Christ built His Kingdom not only in Heaven but on earth? His is the Kingdom of justice, love and truth, the only one where the poor can truly be liberated. Can we rest assured that we help the Church care for those missionaries? Are we not sometimes tempted to pay more attention to organisations no longer willing to spend time on that first stage of liberation: the healing and liberation of souls?

This question is forced upon me when I hear people talk of peasants in developing countries organising themselves in cooperatives or pressure groups. Were they encouraged first to serve and care for the poorest among them, to give them priority? Is their plan for freedom and development based on according privilege to the most oppressed? If not, how will these peasants ever meet Jesus who healed Mary of Magdala?

Somewhere in Africa, way down a trail linking villages despised for their wretchedness and out-of-date beliefs, Mary Magdalene survives on a bed of ashes. Mary Magdalene, to whom Jesus chose to announce the most important tidings that ever would be, since they brought the definite assurance that the poor and all humanity were free. "I am risen from the dead, I go to my Father, go and tell my brothers...." It was from her, a once outcast woman, that the apostles learned the decisive news. She too had eyes that saw not. Like the disciples travelling to Emmaüs, she was unable to recognise Christ. But Jesus chose her. And she had certainly not gone to the tomb by chance. The apostles had hidden behind locked doors, for fear of the Jews. For her, Jesus had been all: her life, her return to the community, her future, her very raison d'être. How could she have helped herself from roaming around the tomb, anxious to embalm His body with loving care?

An unworthy messenger in the eyes of the world, her words hard to believe even for the apostles, it was on her that Christ founded His Church in the world, on that morning of the Resurrection. Just as in our days—of this I feel certain—He builds His Kingdom on an epileptic and cursed woman in a forgotten hamlet somewhere in the African bush. "Mary," says Jesus. And Mary Magdalene, dazzled, recognises Him, "Rabboni!" "Do not come close," He replies. "From now on, our relations have changed, but I shall be with humanity for eternity since for all eternity I shall be with God the Father."

Would there have been another way to allow poor, uneducated and ignorant people to experience the mystery of Jesus dying as a man and rising again as the Son of God? Mary Magdalene, the woman who had been possessed, could now bear witness to

Jesus actually dying on the cross, rising again and going to the Father. She has seen the Lord, He has spoken to her and there she is, vested with her unique role of messenger. She will not convince the apostles, they still need to convince themselves. Yet she will play this essential role entrusted to the outcasts of all times, of unsettling their fellow men, waking them from their languor and inaction.

Did the Evangelist Luke have reasons for identifying Mary of Magdala with the woman who was a sinner and who came to anoint the Lord's feet at the meal in the house of Simon the Leper?

> *A Pharisee invited Jesus to have dinner with him,*
> *and Jesus went to his house and sat down to eat.*
> *In that town was a woman who lived a sinful life.*
> *She heard that Jesus was eating*
> *in the Pharisee's house,*
> *so she brought an alabaster jar full of perfume*
> *and stood behind Jesus, by His feet,*
> *crying and wetting His feet with her tears.*
> *Then she dried His feet with her hair,*
> *kissed them and poured the perfume on them.*
> *When the Pharisee saw this, he said to himself,*
> *"If this man really were a prophet,*
> *He would know who this woman is*
> *who is touching Him;*
> *He would know what kind of sinful life she lives!"*
> *Jesus spoke up and said to him,*
> *"Simon, I have something to tell you."*
> *"Yes, Teacher," he said, "Tell me."*
> *"There were two men*

who owed money to a money-lender,"
Jesus began,
"One owed him five hundred silver coins
and the other one fifty.
Neither of them could pay him back,
so he cancelled the debts of both.
Which one, then, will love him more?"
"I suppose," answered Simon,
"that it would be the one who was forgiven more."
"You are right," said Jesus.
Then He turned to the woman and said to Simon,
"Do you see this woman? I came into your home,
and you gave me no water for my feet,
but she has washed my feet with her tears
and dried them with her hair.
You did not welcome me with a kiss,
but she has not stopped kissing my feet since I
        came.
You provided no olive oil for my head,
but she has covered my feet with perfume.
I tell you, then, the great love she has shown proves
that her many sins have been forgiven.
But whoever has been forgiven little
shows only a little love."
Then Jesus said to the woman, "Your sins are
        forgiven."
The others sitting at the table
began to say to themselves,
"Who is this, who even forgives sins?"
But Jesus said to the woman,
"Your faith has saved you; go in peace."

(Luke 7, 36-50)

If Luke is right, we may be equally overjoyed and amazed to find this woman who was a sinner again at the tomb. She causes me to look at other women I know and whose position as outcasts seems to be irrevocable. Am I far from the truth when I surmise that this woman accused of loose living in Bethany may have been born in poverty? What we know of the lives of women in the Jewish communities of Judea of that time would support this. The average woman was not exposed to the danger of prostitution. But the girls and young widows from poor families certainly were. Born of "impure" women or families, they ran greater risks. Extreme poverty, the difficulty of observing the law, sin, rejection, all form a vicious circle. We noted before that this seems true for all cultures. We see the same in areas of extreme poverty in Europe, Latin America, and in urban districts where the homeless families converge in Africa. It is true even for some much deprived rural communities in different regions and cultures. Was the woman in Bethany another prisoner of such a chain of misfortunes?

At least there is no doubt that she is an outcast. She is despised by those who consider themselves pure. And she shares with all the world's poorest this contempt from those who possess the means to put forward their purity. This contempt confines them all in a state of exclusion, preventing them from acquiring the means to lead an unstained existence. The woman in the Gospel had reached this point. Because she was an alleged sinner, Simon the Leper, Christ's host, would have prevented her from drawing near. So her attempts to be redeemed and her acts of love could bear no fruit. No doubt she was familiar to the house, allowed to cross the threshold, but not to leave the premises pardoned and saved.

Looking at her, I recall what young Jeannine R. had to suffer. She grew up in the promiscuity of a very poor, large family, whose integrity was stubbornly defended by a mother exhausted by illness. In the midst of excessive deprivation, in a hut at the Camp for the Homeless at Noisy-le-Grand, this mother had kept a compelling need for honesty. Her only way to satisfy it was to jealously love and keep close around her the six children. She had entrenched herself as it were, determined to be all and do all for them. No matter how cold the winter, no matter how thread-bare their clothing, she would not go to the town hall nor knock on my door. This desperate clinging to dignity was the only thing she bequeathed to her daughter.

Jeannine loved a neighbour's son, whose family also refused to admit they were poor. Nor did they accept even the smallest offer of help from the neighbours. Jeannine loved Antoine, recognising in him her own pain of having to bear an unacceptable, shameful and yet irremediable condition. But he was not as attached to her as she was to him. Still, she bore him a baby, and soon a second one. But Antoine had other women in the area. He agreed to live with Jeannine, provided she would agree to receive other men. On this point, Jeannine fought her last battle to save the pride inherited from her mother. She finally gave in, but managed to have Antoine set her up in an affluent Paris area with a well-to-do clientele.

When she came to see me, she would talk about the men she now met with all the dignity she could muster. "They are often unhappy. They tell me their worries. Sometimes I don't understand a word. But it doesn't matter. I listen to them and then I feel it is not so much for me that they came, but for the time and attention I give them."

One day she came to see me with a special request. "We're going to get married," she said, "but he refuses to have a church wedding. I would like one, but seeing what I am, I guess I couldn't wear white anyway." Then she took a wedding ring out of her bag and asked me to bless it. "If you bless it, God will still come into our home and it will bring Antoine luck." I promised to bless the ring on the day of her wedding, but that day never came. Antoine was shot and killed shortly afterwards, in a bar at Châlons-sur-Marne.

Jeannine put up another battle to obtain custody of her daughters and retrieve a little money set aside in her mother-in-law's keeping. But with no protection, she lost on both scores. Neither was she allowed to return to her own familiar neighbourhood. She had often come back there, sharing her dresses and money with her sisters and friends. But her mother had died, her father now lived in a trailer, her brothers and sisters had scattered. Her in-laws, still at the Camp, refused to admit her under their roof, but kept her daughters, with the consent of the Social Services. "I'm a disgrace to them all," she said one day. And she was indeed, since she had not disposed of the means to stay true to herself as her mother had. Yet she had shown outstanding constancy in her loves, friendships and personal dignity. Her old neighbours in the Camp used to say that she always knew how to encourage and help, that she was tactful, never hurting or giving offence. How then did it come about that all now looked upon her as a sinner?

Perhaps that question also goes for the woman who was a sinner in Bethany. She too is despised, and yet full of attention to others. Jesus in but a few words establishes a new scale of values around her. As He says, by showing so much love, she makes clear that her sins are already forgiven. Remission is accomplished, she is pure. "For you, Simon," says the Lord, "things are less obvious. Perhaps you are not as free from reproach as you think." We could hear these words from the lips of a poor and humiliated man today, "I entered your house and you did not even pour water on my feet.... You gave me no kiss, you left me at the door and showed me no respect.... You, man without manners who does not comply with the basic rules of hospitality, would you pretend to be giving this woman a lesson?"

I hear the reproach a man in downtown Brussels addresses to a social worker, "You come in without knocking, you do not even say hello, and you start lecturing my wife about the children!" Straight talk which condemns the arrogant today, echoing the words of Jesus in Bethany, more than ever the language of the Son of Man who has seen too much suffering, oppression and hypocrisy to mince His words. As always, He speaks in images so as to be understood not only by Simon but also by Mary

Magdalene. But He is not in a mood to hide His indignation. "You show so little love, do you think you are without blemish before the Lord? What does your purity mean, if it does not spring from overflowing goodness, tact and mercy?" For the people gathered in Simon's house, this was nothing short of overthrowing all traditional rules. "Who is this man who dares remit sins?" Indeed, to forgive sins and restore purity means to overthrow the social hierarchy, elevating the poor who have been kept down on the pretext that they are sinful and impure.

Jesus, undaunted, does not help matters by adding, "Your faith has saved you, go in peace." "Peace," notes the *Traduction Oecuménique* of the Bible, "in the Bible stands for fulness of life, salvation, rather than peace of mind." Mary Magdalene, then, receives a mission: go and lead a new and full life now, living out your love for me and for all. Would Jesus have talked differently if young Jeannine of the Camp of the Homeless, a prostitute in the streets of Paris, could have come to Him? For Simon's guests in the days of Jesus Christ, for the people and social workers around Jeannine today, this reversal of priorities is inconceivable. But the Church must rejoice at finding Mary Magdalene at the tomb as the messenger carrying the news that Christ is risen and that the time of His Church has begun. "I have seen the Lord," she says. "The crucified Rabboni is alive." It will be too hard to believe all at once for the disciples, still deeply grieving. Thomas will refuse to do so, even after their confirmation. He refuses out of fidelity to Jesus, whose ignominious death he so dearly had wished to share. He has too deeply believed in

Jesus giving His life, too ardently wanted to go all the way with Him, too desperately mourned His death to acknowledge, without proof, this other Jesus, risen and returning to His Father. Thomas cannot accept that Jesus' suffering and sacrifice be forgotten so quickly. He needs to touch the wounds in order to be sure that it has not all been a comedy. Jesus understands and anticipates his request: "Put your finger here." But He adds that from now on faith will mean to believe not in Jesus made man and crucified, but in the risen Christ.

This faith, Mary Magdalene, the possessed or perhaps the prostitute, will be the first to receive, and so she will be the first Christian. Her heart, her intuition, all her life's experience tell her: "It is He!" She asks for no proof, she needs none. And it is her example that the whole Church will have to follow, its faith founded in the hearts and the intuition of men and women who will not ask for tangible proof. On the morning of the Resurrection, Mary Magdalene is the first Believer, the first Christian of all time.

CHAPTER TEN

Architects of God's Justice

After triumphing over Satan, Jesus returns from the wilderness "in the power of the Spirit," as says Luke (4, 14). He now sets out to journey through Galilee, soon to preach the Sermon on the Mount. A time for rejoicing has begun, for Jesus plans a fabulous mission for the poor.

"Blessed are the poor in spirit, the meek, those who mourn ... Blessed are those who hunger and thirst for righteousness, blessed are the merciful, the pure in heart ... Blessed are those who create peace ... Blessed are you when people insult you, persecute you and falsely say all kinds of evil because of me. Rejoice and be glad, because great is your reward in Heaven. For in the same way they persecuted prophets who were before

you."(Matthew 5, 11-12)

We had to mingle with the crowds and linger with some of those singled out by Jesus, before meditating on the Beatitudes. We had to get the feeling of the men and women to whom they are addressed for all eternity. For there can be no doubt that the Sermon on the Mount is meant first and foremost for the poor, whose hearts are truly broken and who must keep submissive under oppression. It is meant for the oppressed, who necessarily hunger for justice, for those scorned and insulted by the rich. Christ later will make it plain that all those who divest themselves of their wealth can, of course, join the ranks of the poor. But we have not yet reached that point and should not jostle in the gateway of the Kingdom at the risk of preventing the poor from entering first.

The poor are broken already. As for us, we shall need a lifetime of daily renunciation if we want to become truly like them and one of them. Let us therefore not confuse Christ's priorities, pushing our way inopportunely once more to the front row. "You who are poor are blessed," says Christ. "For you, all the conditions for seeing God and changing the world are fulfilled. For seeing God, first of all, since that requires hearts which refuse division and hatred, oppression and scorn. Your hearts are perfectly prepared. Because of your lot, you know everything about injustice and to what excesses it can lead. You can take full measure of what mercy means, since you must constantly forgive. Therefore, you shall see God, you see Him already in the depth of your being."

191

We are often tempted to say that, to pray to God, we must be in a state of silence and peace. If this were true, God would not be accessible to the poor. He would never show them His face. I see so many mothers constantly hemmed in by the noise, by the neighbours' quarrels, the blare of cars and voices shouting in the street. The children are all over their confined lodgings. Even when they are out, leaving their mother in peace for a while, she is anxious about them. She cannot help but think of their difficulties at school, dreading their coming home in tears because they have been humiliated or beaten up. She worries about the worn-out book bags, the stolen notebooks, the teachers who will scold them for all the things they lack. She knows her husband will soon come home, equally disgusted, perhaps aggressive and without a single word of affection, working off his bitterness on her. What kind of silence can this mother and all these women achieve within their hearts? And for lack of silence, would these women, their husbands and children be deprived of seeing God?

Jesus Christ, through the Beatitudes, restores the truth. He does not simply say, "I am on your side, the Kingdom of my Father will be yours." He declares, "The Kingdom is among you, despite your anxieties and tears, and even because of them." The Beatitudes remind us of the extent to which our own silences can be deceptive, filled with wandering thoughts, but also with misapprehensions. What is the quality of silence in the cloister and in church, if it is not experienced as the silence the poor lack, the silence offered to them through prayer as an essential complement to their lives and efforts? A mother once told me, "You know, I suffered a lot, people have hurt me badly, my children were taken into care. My husband left me, the neighbours jeer at me. Yet I do not hate anybody. I have forgiven them all." She sat there talking to me, and I had a hard time making out what she said. There was the din of the five boys of the man with whom she was now living, neighbours were coming and going, dogs were rummaging everywhere... In the midst of all this unrest, this woman was speaking of forgiveness and peace. Listening to her, I thought of all the silence that nuns must treasure and spread, of all the prayers of priests and of the whole Church which must be filled with silence. But with a silence encompassing the noise of the world. The Church's silent prayer must take charge of all that bars silence and peace of heart and mind for the poor. To whom should this prayer be addressed, if not to the Saviour who chose to live among them, there where silence is always broken, where hearts are always laden and thoughts always troubled?

What use is silent worship if it does not ensure that the Lord can dwell in the hearts of the poor, in their hectic lives, in their ever-restless minds? The well-off are often preoccupied, but their worries are not comparable to those of the wretched. The latter know all the time that they will lack essentials, that they will have to scrounge, invent or beg and implore to survive. We sometimes speak of the survival strategies of the poor, without always realising that these drain all their energies and attention. These strategies leave the poor no moment of respite. Yet

God dwells within them, the gates of the Kingdom are open to them. This was so in Galilee, but Christ had to come in order to lead the crowd to a halt, to a great moment of rejoicing when all would be told, "You are not impure, not unworthy, just the opposite! God is among you. He is part of you who are continually in need. Powerless and ever at the mercy of others, you are constantly being purified and therefore pardoned and blessed. In choosing me, you have chosen wisely, for you and I are building the Kingdom. All that you experience makes you its leading architects."

"Builders of the Kingdom," say the Beatitudes, but also builders of justice on earth. "You will not only inherit the earth tomorrow, you can inherit it now, creating change in the world today. Your suffering under oppression, your pain under persecution, can force humanity to change, to look at the world in a new way, to be indignant with injustice and to tolerate it no longer—on condition, of course, that you give new significance to your own existence, seeing it no longer as fatal or as a punishment, but as a covenant with God and a point of departure for renewal. You must have the will to set out for this renewal and choose it freely."

The Beatitudes are in no way soothing. They do not lull the poor into passivity. The words "because of me" and the reference to the Prophets reveal their mobilising character. They bestow on the poor a mission on earth. To suffer in the name of justice means to suffer for human rights and for a society that will respect them. "The Kingdom," says Jesus, "begins in the hearts of people." But "a good tree cannot bear bad fruit" (Matthew 7, 19) and "not everyone who says to me 'Lord, Lord' will enter the Kingdom, but only those who do the will of my Father who is in Heaven" (Matthew 7, 21). What is the Father's will? The instructions Jesus gives after proclaiming the Beatitudes represent a masterly declaration of the unity, universality and eternity of the Kingdom. Piety of heart toward God and social justice among men and women are inextricably linked. We cannot pretend to detect different levels, nor can we ignore the guidelines for political action.

In any case, it was to the crowds in poverty that Christ announced that He had come not to abolish the law but to fulfil it. And the law governed social structures as well as religious obligations. Protection of life and the bonds of marriage, the basis for swearing oaths, the laws of retaliation and of truce, peace, the manner of almsgiving (which we call social assistance today), the role of money and consequently of economic endeavour, the concern for the future which leads to profit-making, savings, hoarding and undue reserves. . . , touching upon these many basic questions meant that Jesus was directly concerned with the organisation of society. He drew up a balance sheet without distinguishing between religious, social and economic affairs. Rules for spiritual life and those governing social relations intermingle and are presented as an overall pattern based on the will of God. Here and now, the Kingdom is being built, love, prayer and mercy bearing the fruits of justice on earth.

Perhaps people who do not crave justice in this world can imagine a dividing line between the justice of God and justice of humanity. For Fourth World families, as no doubt for the poor of all times, such a distinction seems unthinkable. It cannot exist. Christ says, "Do unto others as you would have them do unto you. That is the meaning of the Law and the Prophets." For the very poor, this is not just a guideline for personal conduct, but a blueprint for society. They suffer too much from established social structures. To them, what individual people are called upon to do for one another will necessarily overthrow this iniquitous social order. Perhaps the poor also realise better than others the price to be paid for such a profound change both in people and structures?

The poor themselves will have to make a considerable effort to become liberators, to renew bonds among themselves and to present themselves in a new light to the world. Even as a young boy growing up in broken-down housing in the Rue Saint Jacques, I never imagined that God or the Church would invite me to remain inactive. On the contrary, it seemed to me that, to live the Gospel, everything must change, in my mother's life, in the neighbourhood, in our relations with the better-off. And I felt I had to contribute to this change myself. I could not even see who would bring it about besides the poor themselves. The Beatitudes therefore seemed to me to be Christ's commitment to us. "The Romans, Herod's henchmen, the Pharisees, all consider you inferior. Yet, you are the chosen children of the Father and if you fight for justice, He is with you. For there is no love without justice." I always believed I could hear Christ encouraging us, "If you take the pains, if you truly believe you can win, not for yourselves, but for all the others, then you will win."

Fourth World families, however, taught me little by little how difficult it can be to think oneself capable of standing upright, of fighting and winning when one has always been despised. By virtue of what conviction or hope would they transform themselves into builders of the Kingdom, when all their experience had taught them to keep quiet, to huddle up and close themselves off? "Me, I keep quiet," said Mr. Lebrun. "In this area, you'd better go unnoticed." After a lifetime of wandering from slum to shantytown, from emergency shelter to slum, he is settled at last in a village in Normandy. Part of his family, children and grandchildren, have been reassembled around him. His wife still finds it a little hard not to seek forgetfulness in drink. The grandchildren require special tutoring at school. Some nuns nearby, in the face of the family's poverty, have turned to old customs still to be found in the countryside; they take care of the children's clothing. Mr. Lebrun, while keeping quiet, does not necessarily manage to go unnoticed. Yet this has been his guideline all through life. The people gossip in the village, while in his kitchen through an old-fashioned pair of spectacles he strains to spell out the Gospel. Are we to believe that Christ asks this wretched man of seventy to stand and bear witness?

We are to believe it. Mr. Lebrun has sent us a message. He wishes to marry, before God, the woman who has shared his existence. She has given him seven children and they suffered indescribable misery together. For years, his companion has stood over the family threshold forming a veritable barricade. Behind her, the floor of her Nissen hut was strewn with mattresses, a few stools, a stove—never a piece of real furniture. In a saucepan on the ground I would notice leftover potatoes to be reheated for the children's supper. No outsiders were allowed to see this wretchedness. "If they did, what would happen to the children? The police would come and take them away," Madame Lebrun used to say.

In 1984, the Lebruns have a house from which they can no longer be evicted. They have decided to get married in the church. However, the local priest hesitates to give them the sacrament. The whole village is by now discussing the problem and Mr. Lebrun has called for me urgently. He does not ask to be enabled to put things straight at this late stage in life so that he may die in peace. Simply, while spelling out the Gospel through his worn-out glasses, he has become convinced that he owes it to God and to his wife to marry her. He therefore will be obliged to do something contrary to his entire life's philosophy, namely to draw attention to himself! Indeed, Mr. Lebrun makes himself the laughing-stock of the village and a cause of bewilderment for the diocese. But at the age of seventy, Christ has called him, asking for this inner revolution "because of me."

While Mr. Lebrun, recognising himself in the Gospel, has become a witness of God in his own way, his youngest daughter has joined a training programme to become an ATD Fourth World militant. I do not know what she thinks of God. All I can say is that as a little girl in the Camp for the Homeless in

Noisy-le-Grand, she loved her family and the people around her. Attending school irregularly, like the other girls her age, she soon became a street child and part of a gang, since at home all she could do was sit or lie on a mattress to eat or sleep. In the midst of this promiscuity and violence, Danièle, by an uncommon grace, learned to love her milieu. Even as a child she always had an excuse ready to defend her family or her gang. She bristled at the slightest disparaging remark about her mother's rough countenance. Today, the same loyalty pushes her to learn to write, to speak in public and to represent all Fourth World families. As I saw her grow, I kept on thinking that the eyes of the Virgin Mary must rest on her.

The Mother of God needed no inner revolution. She had God, the poor, and justice enshrined in her heart from birth. Danièle also loved and defended her own since early childhood. But not all women who live in wretchedness are so fortunate. All are blessed in the sense of the Beatitudes. They must, however, summon up their courage, resist the temptation to let themselves be engulfed by extreme poverty, make monumental efforts to strengthen their love of others and their own self-esteem. At times, they manage to do so, they stand upright, they press the parish priest to baptise their children, they go to family meetings or to the ATD Fourth World People's University. Then again, they stand up no longer, they seem to lay down their arms, they withdraw from all activities. Some return much later; some give up for good. They have lost faith in their struggle. The goal is too remote, the burden of scorn and malicious gossip too heavy. "I am tired," says Madame Lachaud. "I am ill and anyway I have my own life to live."

Who will tell Mme. Lachaud that to "live her own life" is precisely to set herself free by liberating all those families around her who are even poorer than she is? Who goes around the St. Jacques district where I grew up, who goes to the Garenne district, to the tenements of the Parc and to St. Léonard, who goes to tell all the poor around the Cathedral of Angers today, "Blessed are you, the architects of change"? Who will remind them, "You are seated highest at the table, for what you say about justice, truth and peace is vital"? When Christ returns, will He still find people who bring to the poor the good news that the earth is already theirs? People who tell them that their life experience can change people's hearts and force humanity to exact just laws? He Himself said just this: "You can oblige people to do this if you take sufficient pains. You will force them to pray to the Father in a different way because they will have made room for the most cruelly crucified among His children." But I no longer hear Christians say, "You are blessed" to the children who go to school with their stomachs empty, to the families living in slums or tents, in shanties or caravans, or to those who must seek shelter from the Salvation Army. These very poor people who are supposed to lack a sense of politics, and on behalf of whom many pretend to change the world without even consulting them, what else can they do but abstain from all struggles, since we no longer proclaim their true identity as the builders of justice?

Yet, the deep poverty that prevents people from

going to the Temple or to church, from feeling at ease with those who do, does not destroy their awareness that God has not rejected them. But the poor, who are always pushed back to the last row, need to be reassured through the Beatitudes that they hold a preferential role in the Father's plan. They have the right to be told. They were no more blessed by right in the days of Jesus than they are now. The crowd around Jesus on the Mount *became* blessed because Jesus announced to them that they were. "Because of Jesus," because He had revealed Himself to them and because they had believed in Him. They were reborn from then on, because they could give a new sense to their state of poverty. This is how the Sermon on the Mount became all at once an explosion of joy and the beginning of a mission. Without the rejoicing because all could see themselves as children of God, the mission would have been frightening. I sometimes feel that, though we may still remember the mission, we have forgotten that, in the eyes of Jesus, it had to be linked with festivity, with the elation of forgiveness and the security of knowing one is loved by the Father. Jesus knew how hard it would be for the poor to see themselves no longer as contemptible sinners, incapable and insignificant. Only God could change this image and restore the truth. Without God, the enthusiasm would soon wane, the perspective of having a mission and being up to it would dim. The priests and Pharisees would not be long in wiping them out. They had never before failed to smother the poor.

"And the people were astonished by His doctrine," says Matthew, concluding his account of the

Sermon. Were they stunned, taken aback? Perhaps they were, but they must have been astonished with happiness and wonder. No doubt the road would be no less strewn with obstacles. "Straight is the gate and narrow is the way which leadeth unto life." Christ says so. He never made misleading promises. "The road will not be easier than before. There will be false prophets to misdirect you. But unlike yesterday, you now know where you are going and you will follow the road with gladness and lightness of heart in the company of the prophets. For you are, like the prophets before you, the messengers of God." In contemplating Jesus surrounded by the crowd on the mountainside, I wonder once more what brings us to our present-day ideas on revolution and liberation. What room do they leave for forgiveness and rejoicing? Who tells the poor today, "You are the salt of the earth, you are the light of the world. Consequently we, the haves, are not coming to dictate, nor to impose a programme on you that you have not drafted yourselves. We are here to listen to you, reminding you that it was Christ in poverty who sketched your plan, declaring you blessed for being the first to carry it out."

I wonder whether we take the full measure of the responsibility Christ entrusted to the poor in handing over to them the Kingdom, the Law and the Prophets. They will have to put the Beatitudes into effect among themselves first of all. Let us look once more at this crowd at Jesus' feet. Most of them are poor, but they are neither a homogeneous nor a united people. Some work, others are unemployed or underemployed. Beside them are the very poorest, the crippled, incapable of being useful, the lepers who frighten those around them, abandoned women without a home to shelter them, the blind punished by God, beggars in great numbers. . . . There must have been many thieves as well. In this most motley crowd, what does it mean to be blind in a family of donkey or camel drivers, to be a leper among those who collected the excrements of dogs, or among the tanners using this impure substance in their trade? What does it mean to be a beggar, in the eyes of small pedlars who have little left to peddle and whose clientele shrinks as compulsory surrender of the soil proceeds, the threat of sinking into beggary themselves too close for comfort? Even among the Galileans, generally disdained by Jerusalem's wealthy, there are families considered pure and honourable. This is true for Jesus' family, of the House of David.

Many others were highly respected, priests or Pharisees or those holding other respected occupations handed down from father to son. Beside them existed the mass of impure families, among whom were those who held despised trades, most of them occupations of the poor. If these families brought into the world an epileptic or deaf-mute son, if the daughter of a camel-driver became a prostitute, mothering illegitimate children, what kind of social stratification, what further disunion could result from this? The family of Simon the Leper could afford to have a son who was a leper. They could even help him get cured and take his place again within the community, in a position to offer hospitality to Christ.

Having solved his problems, he could look down on the woman who came to pour costly ointment on Jesus' feet. When he was still a leper, did he sit with other lepers, sons of tanners, of shepherds or of women of easy conduct? It is unlikely. I feel I have never yet totally grasped what must have been the diversity even among the poor of Jesus' day.

Yet, to contemplate Christ and hear His teaching, we must be able to see the people around Him individually, listening to Him through many different ears. We must be able to see the hands stretched out to Him, so unlike one another. Some have been shaped by a trade, others are deformed by illness. Some tremble or cannot even really reach out. The voices crying out to Jesus are just as dissimilar. That of the beggar cannot be mistaken for that of the pedlar or of the farmer growing his corn. All humanity, especially all humanity in poverty, is assembled at Christ's feet at the hour of the Beatitudes. What an opportunity to observe this crowd, if only we knew how to use our eyes.

"It is among you, people in poverty and yet so different from one another, that the Kingdom begins," says Jesus. "Let your light shine before men, that they may see your good works, and glorify your Father which is in Heaven." (Matthew 5, 16) To establish God's justice among themselves is no light task. Yet this will be their only way of rendering themselves credible before humanity. The assignment is far more important than anyone could have foreseen. Peasant families will have to invent new relationships with the despised families of launderers. Small winegrowers struggling to maintain their farm must organise themselves in good harmony with landless labourers. Shopkeepers will have to care for their own invalids but equally for those of the infinitely worse-off stonecutters. Sons of pure families will have to reach out to the paralytics among the impure, to teach foreigners, to protect women whose honour is blemished.

Christ can proclaim so far-reaching a revolution among the poor because He has accomplished it in His own life. As the son of a poor but pure family, He has not kept His distance from the wretched. Had He done so, He might still have been credible in the eyes of the wealthy, but He would not have convinced the crowd on the mountain. "Judge not, that you be not judged." "Be not unbending, forgetting man in the name of rules and norms." "Do not be fickle; keep your word to one another." "You have been taught, 'An eye for an eye and a tooth for a tooth.' Do not believe it. Only mercy and forgiveness will lead you to greatness and respectability." All this is much to ask of the poor, and Jesus asks even more. Not only will they have to forgive, but they should suffer with those who have wished them evil and tainted their honour or damaged the little security they had so painfully acquired. In short, they must use their own state of poverty to liberate those even more oppressed than themselves. You, the poor, says Jesus, will have to make sure of your own rights, but even more of the rights of those more forsaken than you. You will not swerve from their side as would the New Rich, the new holders of power. Your first and foremost intent will be to obtain justice for your neighbour. You shall accept being persecuted because of me, and because of the most miserable at your side. Only the most downtrodden can uphold your sense of combat, your sense of the Kingdom which begins here and now.

In the light of the Beatitudes, poverty must become the tool for creating the festivity and the joy of change henceforth ensured to those who resided in utter darkness. Jesus reminds us all that the blessed cannot fight like pagans. The pagans, He says, have forgotten that their struggles must benefit all people. Taking advantage of the trust of others, they have gained wealth and prestige at the expense of the poor. If the latter allow themselves to be similarly trapped, detaching themselves from their own and creating an entourage that screens them off, they will no longer understand justice as they do now. Their struggle will be different and will lose its credibility. To build the Kingdom, the poor have no choice but to remain gentle, humble and to refuse to enrich themselves.

Jesus never ceased repeating this: "Your poverty must be transformed into dynamism and also into joy. If you become hard and aggressive to those around you, your fight will have lost its very purpose. If you lose your gladness, you are no longer fighting for the poorest. You are no longer defending your neighbour. Whatever you may achieve in my name and in the name of the wretched does not belong to you. Nothing you gain should serve to make a name for yourselves. Never mistake the success of the community for your personal triumph. The red carpet, the fanfare, the palaces, they are not for you. Temples built in my name must never be a means to push yourselves forward. The only record you must leave to history should be that of your love of God and of your neighbours. The only rule for organising society is 'love one another' and share both your sorrows and your victories."

I can bear witness that Christ's teaching remains valid in the areas of extreme poverty today. "You will be seated first at the table, for it is you who ask for respect and dignity most desperately." Fourth World families understand that things cannot be otherwise. That Jesus should call them blessed is a joyful discovery, but one that does not surprise them. "If Jesus visited our tenement, imagine what a party we'd have!" In this light it also becomes possible to envisage the incalculable responsibility: "Astonish the world by establishing God's justice among you. You, who hardly have the strength to stand on your feet, get up. You, who go through life your shoulders bowed, stand tall."

The wretched, liberating those more miserable than themselves, the poor liberating the poorest among them, those who hunger for justice acting and suffering for those even more starved than they, Jesus' teaching keeps its full meaning today. I see no other way, if something must truly change in the relationship between rich and poor. For the poor to create justice among themselves seems the only way to finally put the rich in their proper place. If the poor thus become the "light of the world," they need no longer submit to the law of the rich. The roles will be reversed at last, the rich having to participate in the projects of the poor, to ask to be allowed to work with them, and having to learn to do so. Such a thing was unheard of in Jesus' day and still is now. We never envisage the poor as living in the city on the hill to which all eyes must turn. We still see them as those who must be taught by others. Even Jesus' life and sacrifice do not always seem to suffice to make us understand the source of the light, who are the pupils and perhaps the servants. Yet the Beatitudes are perfectly clear on these questions.

For Christians, at any rate, through the Beatitudes the world is changed, roles are clarified, all things take their proper place. It is true that we remain in the presence of a mystery far too deep to fathom. The mystery of God who makes His grace penetrate the world through the lowliest of His children. If this does not yet change our structures, it transforms our hearts, reduces us to silence, leads us to contemplation and prayer. It is no longer our privilege to create new structures, certainly not for the poor and even less in their name. They are the light at which we must kindle our lanterns. We are obliged to go to them and to share with them their concern for the most wretched at their side. We must become their servants and pupils, so reminding the poor that they are blessed. They were blessed, they still are, provided we go tell them so.

The other day in the Netherlands, I listened to a group of Fourth World families converse with a member of the European Parliament. The families told of their efforts to maintain a holiday farm for the most impoverished among them. All these families try to contribute to its maintenance and management. They assemble means for entertainment, organise musical events, collect books and games for the children. The member of parliament listened with an air of pity and finally cut them short. "That's all good and well," she said, "but what you really need is a change of structures. Your holiday farm is very nice but it changes nothing. To change your existence, you must use the ballot-box." One father insisted, asking whether it was fair that the government refuse to subsidise their farm. "That is not the question," replied the member of parliament. "The important thing is to vote for a different government." "But," the man persisted, "you agree that we cannot count on politicians." The conversation ended there, the representative reminding us, as she left, that these families still had a lot to learn. Yet, who must teach whom, who are the masters and who should be the servants? Do we know how to find and how to listen to the masters?

Through the Beatitudes in the Sermon on the Mount, Jesus Christ does not call upon the haves to liberate the have-nots. Neither does He call upon the poor to overthrow the rich. He enjoins *all* to liberate humanity together. There can be but one Kingdom, one justice uniting all people. But the poor will be recognised as the first architects. This means a reversal almost too hard to accept. It baffles us, despite our belief in human rights. Should we really admit that the poor should be in the service of the poorest and dictate to us the ways to justice? They who have hardly been to school? Can we conceive of justice as ascending to us from the very bottom of the social scale, from the very depths of misery? All this seems exaggerated. When turning our eyes to the poor and the miserable, would we no longer be looking in the gutter, but toward the city on the hill? This is difficult to comprehend. "Do not let yourselves be called teachers," is surely one of the most inconceivable precepts for the scribes, the doctors of law, the learned of all times.

"What is the most important thing to learn?" an ATD Fourth World team asked some of the poorest children on the Lower East Side of Manhattan. "Give us a computer," they answered. Extremely poor parents in France echo their request, "What our children need is electronics. Nowadays, that's all that counts." This demand seems to encircle the globe. It comes to us from a shantytown in Haïti. A Fourth World team brings books and knowledge to the hillocks there. "Teach us to use a computer," clamour the children who do not even know what it is to have running water or regular schooling. We pass on their message to an institution for public aid to development: "Help us provide computers for some of the poorest children in the world." "This is a premature request," the official experts decide. In France, in 1983, others had answered à similar proposal almost likewise: "How can we put computers in classrooms of retarded children? We have not yet provided our regular high schools with computers!" Thus the scribes continue to decide for the poor. How can they give up the privilege of being called teachers? And how can they abstain from deciding in favour of their own children first?

No wonder Christ asked the poor to be as transparent as He was Himself, their deeds as convincing as His own. "Because of me," for the love of Him and not for the mere satisfaction of creating a new system. Experts will certainly establish new structures, but it is not from them that the city on the hill will draw its light. Light will be kindled only by love, and that love will have to be strong. For the poor must necessarily move forward against the current and they will always be in danger of getting battered or being misled. The parables on the Kingdom are perfectly clear to them on this score. May they at least be united by bonds of love. "Be perfect, as your Heavenly Father is perfect."

"Blessed are those who mourn. . . those who hunger. . . the merciful. . . " The poor will have to repeat this to themselves over and over. Just as they must remember that justice without love and mercy which include all humanity is a snare and a mirage. They must be sure of this in order to remain firm. Only love and faith in Jesus Christ can maintain the inspiration and joy, since He achieved the impossible.

On the mountainside, through the Beatitudes, Christ shook the world's order for all time to come.

CHAPTER ELEVEN

"Take Courage and Do Not Fear, It Is I"

Our way of reading the Gospel helps us to recognise the Saviour made man in poverty in all His majesty. What place does it leave to the more fortunate in this world? "If the poor are the Church, then what are we who are rich?" a friend asked me. "Would we not also be the Church?" another wrote to me. It seems to me the main question is not whether we are the Church, but whether we love the Church of the poor, the Church of Christ in misery. Do we love her with all our strength? Are we committed, devoting our lives to her? If so, the question whether we are the Church becomes pointless. We belong to her, we declare ourselves her children, children of God. Would our Holy Mother

Church deny us when God Himself does not?

Yet, we must never forget that Jesus Christ loves all people. He loves them because they are human beings. The Gospel does not grant to all the same role in God's plan. But we each have an indispensable part to play. The Gospel, it is true, does overflow with the tenderness of Jesus for the very poorest. But what would this tenderness mean, if from the most wretched upward it did not engulf all the other children of the Father? God's love does not separate people; it can only unify them. God brings together those who were estranged, that they may build the Kingdom as one. In the Gospel, all men and women are assembled, although all do not walk the same path toward this land of unity.

The difference between the poor and the wealthy is that Christ tells the poor to transform their condition by using their very poverty, whereas the rich must renounce their condition altogether. "If any would come after me, they must deny themselves and take up their crosses and follow me." (Matthew 16, 24) "Any," says Christ, and consequently *all* people are called upon to follow Him. The difference lies in the cross each one must take up. The cross of the poor will not be that of the wealthy and the educated, while the most downtrodden are already burdened with so heavy a cross that Christ has come to carry it with them.

The cross of the poor is that they must dare stand up and act as the blessed ones, fully accepting their poverty-stricken milieu, when they would prefer to remain unobtrusive and close themselves off. The cross of the rich is the contrary: making themselves humble instead of being in charge, and agreeing to leave their familiar milieu when they would rather hold their place there. They must first quell in themselves the question of the sons of Zebediah, who wanted to seat one at the right and one at the left hand of the Master in His glory (Mark 10, 35-38). Instead, they will become servants, ranking with the lowest.

*You know that those
who are regarded as rulers of the Gentiles
lord it over them
and their high officials exercise authority over them.
But it shall not be so among you:
but whosoever will be great among you
must be your servant
and whoever wants to be first must be slave of all.
For even the Son of Man
did not come to be served,
but to serve and to give His life
as a ransom for many.*

(Mark 10, 42-45)

For the rich, giving their lives in ransom for all really means abandoning all they have acquired, that it may serve the poor. Jesus could not have offered them a more exalting mission. By bringing their fullest potentials, their whole selves, and their communities to flourish for the benefit of the multitude, they will enrich humanity more than anyone can imagine. A truly magnificent task is thus entrusted to them.

I am deeply convinced that Jesus Christ loved the

rich who were around Him. He honoured them as much as He honoured the poor. They too were to have their unique task in the sculpting of justice. If the Beatitudes were addressed to the poor, was not the Last Judgment a solemn promise made to the rich who would divest themselves of their possessions?

> *Then the King will say to those on His right,*
> *"Come, you who are blessed by my Father.*
> *Take your inheritance, the Kingdom*
> *prepared for you since the creation of the world.*
> *For I was hungry and you gave me something to*
>   *eat,*
> *I was thirsty and you gave me drink,*
> *I was a stranger and you invited me in,*
> *I was threadbare and you gave me clothes,*
> *I was ill and you tended me,*
> *I was imprisoned and you visited me."*
> *Then the righteous will answer Him,*
> *"Lord, when did we see You hungry and feed You,*
> *or thirsty and give You drink?*
> *When did we see You a stranger and ask You in,*
> *or needing clothes and clothed You?*
> *When did we see You ill or in prison and go to visit*
>   *You?"*
> *The King will reply, "I tell you the truth,*
> *whatever you did for the least of these children of*
>   *mine,*
> *you did for me."*

(Matthew 25, 34-40)

"For the least of these children of mine," says Jesus, and we cannot doubt whom He meant. The crowd is still there and He is not in the habit of confusing the poor and the totally excluded. "The least of my children" was not a figure of speech to Him. Christ always points to real people whose faces are there to be seen by all. Faces that could be frightening. Jesus honours the rich with His confidence that they can overcome their fright. To them too, He extends His tenderness. The whole Gospel seems meant to reassure them, "I tell you the truth, it is hard for a rich man to enter the Kingdom of Heaven. With human beings this is impossible, but with God all things are possible." (Matthew 19, 23-26) I feel these words hold both a promise and a mystery. Rich, you will be unable to enter, but stripped of your wealth it becomes possible. I tell you no more in the name of my Father. He, for His part, can disavow none of His children. Know that, to Him, everything remains possible. As for me, I tell you: strip yourself of your possessions and enter; I await you eagerly.

This offer honours the rich because it is monumental. Like the poor, they will have to overcome considerable fear and uncertainty. They will need encouragement. I cannot help thinking of them when I hear these words: "'It's a ghost!' they said, crying out in fear. But Jesus immediately said to them, 'Take courage and do not fear, it is I.'" Even Peter asked for a sign. "'Lord, if it is you, tell me to come to you on the water.' 'Come,' He said." (Matthew 14, 26-30) Peter will come and walk on the water as long as he trusts in the Lord. When his fear returns, he sinks. I think of the rich called upon to turn to the poorest who, from the depths of their tenements and settlements, appear to them like frightening shadows of humanity. They must go into streets and areas where they never dreamt of going. In the presence of those who live there, I have seen so many men and women thunderstruck, having to overcome their disbelief that Christ could have chosen as His companions people so disfigured by extreme deprivation. They had thought the poor were different—more educated, polite, grateful. They had hoped they would be more welcoming. They have the right to be reassured, convinced that by going to the poorest, they are going toward Christ and will be the beloved of the Father. Jesus makes them this mysterious gift: what you do to the least of my children, you do to me. Even if you did not recognise me, if you loved them and served them, you will be beloved. This mystery of the solidarity among God's people is entrusted by Christ to the rich. If your heart guides you to the poorest, you are a party to the Covenant, whether or not you are aware of it.

Jesus goes further and tells the rich they cannot be spared in the Covenant. He criticised the Pharisees for preventing the poor from entering the Kingdom because they could have made them enter. Jesus lamented, "But you unfortunates, you, the rich ... you who have been sated ... you who laugh now ...", because the rich could and should live otherwise. Alas! Unfortunate and wretched are you when, by your way of life, you bring sorrow upon the poor. Jesus did not curse the rich, He lamented over them. I needed you, you were essential to me for achieving the Kingdom. . . The very poor themselves lament in this way every day of their lives; I need them and they disappoint me.

I never could believe that Jesus' conversations with the Pharisees, the priests or the Sadduceans were mere polemics. Nor do I think they were condemnations. Christ never treated anyone as either an object or a person condemned. Even on the Cross, He asked God to forgive all. He asked this in His own name, but also, no doubt, in the name of the penitent thief at His side. He knew that the well-off were also capable of believing in Him and He never ceased telling them so. As He said to Nicodemus, "You should not be surprised at my saying, 'You must be born again'. . ." For God loved the world enough to give His one and only son so that whoever believes in Him shall not perish but shall have eternal life. For God did not send His son into the world to condemn the world but to save the world through Him." (John 3, 7 and 16-17)

To this man of mature years, a Pharisee come to see Him under cover of night, Jesus explains that God does not wage a partisan war. No human being may be allowed to perish. But it is not enough that you believe in me, Nicodemus. You must also become a new man, leading a new life. God needs you. "But whoever lives by the truth comes into the light, so that it may be seen plainly that what he has done has been done through God." (John 3, 21) God needs all men and women, and it seems to me that Christ confirms this through all His preaching. "If you want to be perfect, go, sell your possessions and give to the poor, and you will have treasure in Heaven." (Matthew 19, 21) Is that all He wishes to say to the rich young man? By no means! "Then follow me," He adds. Follow me, not as part of my court or retinue, but because I need you.

When announcing the Last Judgment, Jesus reminds us one last time. "They will go, . . . the just, into eternal life." The rich can become just; they can under certain conditions. They must no longer draft grand projects for a society that serves their own interests, nor take the lead of powerful political movements in order to achieve personal glory and privilege. That is not what it means to follow Christ. On the contrary. "Here is my servant whom I have chosen, the one I love, in whom I delight. He will not quarrel or cry out, no one will hear his voice in the streets, till he leads justice to victory. In his name, the nations will put their hope." (Matthew 12, 18-21) This too is meant literally.

"The nations," and consequently the poor, have more trust in God than in humanity. They hope for God's justice rather than for the world's. The rich must know this and Christians learn from it. Christ does not ask them to invent new ways of conducting world affairs nor to wage battles in the name of the oppressed. That would be another way to stay on top. Jesus invites them to achieve with Him the total revolution which consists of proclaiming that the poor are the light of the world. He asks them to act accordingly. The light will no longer come only from the rich, and they will no longer have a monopoly on knowledge. They will have to learn other ways of running the world, leadership will be lost to them, they will have to make themselves pupils and servants of justice.

Throughout the centuries, people have no doubt found convenient interpretations of the Gospel. In our own days, we have learnt to translate Christ's concrete and precise precepts into increasingly abstract terms. But the poor have no means to do so, and I doubt that they would wish it. Our compromises with the Gospel are rarely in their favour. Jesus, moreover, is one of them, and they feel that our interpretations do Him no justice. This is unquestionably so for the very poorest who are offended as is Jesus Christ Himself by our slightest infidelities. Our circumventions and half-measures never remain hidden from them long. They are the catalysts who reveal the truth. Is this not why so many files on Fourth World families are shunted from bureau to bureau with no result? No one can acquiesce to what they ask, yet no one dares admit failure by saying no. When a civil servant finally refuses the request, he does so vehemently, "You have no valid claim, you have no right to ask this..." To force the poor to prove their rights again and again is the most devious way of preventing them from making the light of truth shine out over what our communities, our society, our systems, organisations and movements are really worth. We present these as standards to which the poor must conform. We can allow ourselves to do so on the basis of an unfortunate arrangement made with the Gospel: Christ was poor, but not wretched. This allows us to recognise service to the poor as obligatory, while service to the wretched remains optional, a special vocation, maybe a marginal one. Christ and the very poorest ask us to renounce such a compromise.

In any case, no half-measure will ever bear the scrutiny of the excluded. In their presence, we cannot for long claim to be slaves, as was our Lord, if we are not devoted to them body and soul. We will never convince them of our devotion to Christ. We will be unable to declare them blessed in His name, if we ourselves do not believe it so intensely that we reorganise our existence accordingly. Yet this is precisely Christ's appeal: Go tell it to the poorest, above all. Leave everything behind to reveal the news to them!

I hear the same appeal from so many mothers, telling me over the years, "My sin, Father, is to have brought wretched children into the world." "What I did wrong was to have children condemned to live in misery." These women were waiting for me to answer them, "This is not so, for you have loved them! Your children are not only the flesh of your flesh, they are also the tenderness of your daily love, of this love which costs you so very much." They had an inexpressible need to hear that, even if their children had different fathers, what really counted were the risks and pain their mother had endured for them. "Your children do not have all they need, but they have a mother who thinks of a thousand ways to keep food on their plates, a mother who runs right and left to scrounge some clothes so they may go to school." I often had to insist that they were not guilty, or unworthy of loving God, and that they could pray without fear.

Throughout my priesthood, Fourth World families waited for me to tell them they need not torture themselves this way, since God loved them. When I was younger, this used to surprise me. In fact, people asked me to prove that God loved them. I constantly had to remind them of the signs which said that the Lord was with them and would not forsake them. I pointed to the children coming home, not in tears, but smiling and hugging them, to the next-door neighbour come to share some vegetables just found cheap at the market, to the postman bringing the long-awaited child benefit allowance cheque, or to the husband who had found a few days' work. The often unpredictable signs of love, to be seized as they come. Signs which also were multiplied and disseminated, so great was the need to pass on to others the sudden happiness. "I just received the arrears on my children's allocation, I must run to tell the neighbours." "My husband found a job, setting up the market stalls and taking them down at night. The kids will be happy and Gino will get his anorak at last!" So God was not only a God for oneself, but the God of all. And it was essential that He be revealed in these settlements of misery. It is even more so now that lifetime unemployment has set in.

How often must I repeat to these men worn out with frustration, "Do understand why your neighbour drinks and lashes out at you. Be on his side, try to protect him when he wants to fight. For you know full well that he is completely discouraged." Over and over, the same message must be spread: "Stand by that man who suffers, because then Christ is in you." But to bear witness to God, I must witness daily existence and know how to read the events of these lives. To encourage them to transcend themselves, we must surpass ourselves together. In order to help them develop experience and intuition into understanding and judgment, I must work with them on more coherent thinking about God and life, about humanity and love. This is what Jesus Christ did with the poor and He asks me to do likewise.

Jesus also commanded the rich to go tell the poor and the rejected that they had a contribution of primary importance to offer the world. The extremely poor are blessed, not because they attend the feast, but because they have an indispensable part to play there. The rich must learn to recognise this part, and they must therefore be present. If not, how will they understand what it means to be solely and totally human because one has been stripped of all means to put up a front, to wrap oneself in enhancing roles and situations? The poor live the truth about humanity in its barest form. They, therefore, possess an acute sense of reality. For them, life does not consist of words, of ideological conjectures, nor of grand political projects. They have no such abstractions to which to resort. The only thing that matters is daily life, the love of the children, keeping the family together against all odds, the dignity of holding a useful job. They try to safeguard these essentials with a thousand small gestures that will somehow make things work despite everything: a mother going hungry for several days so that her sons might go to the movies; a man bringing home a rusty, but still serviceable stove, found while rummaging in the dumps. . . . In the eyes of Christ, the poor are fortunate, because they have a real understanding of these things. They cultivate these tiny gestures not to survive, but to live. All the poor seek is to surpass mere survival, and to achieve this they never cease inventing concrete gestures, thereby creating realities in the midst of daily existence. This is how they stand up against adversity, illness, contempt. Not through ideas and flowery language, but through deeds. These deeds, in truth, carry hope for the poor themselves and for all humanity. We must learn to interpret them and thereby to measure the distance we have taken ourselves from life's realities.

This distance is incalculable, but only the poor are aware of this. As I said, they are rarely mistaken about the people they meet. We are more easily deceived. We have organised ourselves as civil servants of life, arming ourselves with preconceived ideas, regulations, certificates and standards. These protect us from people who do not suit us because they live, think and suffer differently from us. Our confinement to this way of administering life blinds us to the pain of the rejected. Thus their suffering is compounded by the additional contempt shown for their courage in resisting adversity. The poor are not people who have given up. Even the very poorest are loath to submit. Even the paralytic at the pool of Bethesda had not let himself die after thirty-eight years of shattered hopes. How deep an abyss separates us from the poor when we imagine them apathetic, parasites by choice whose evil propensities we should counteract! It seems a terrifying way to convince ourselves that we are always right. Right in our struggles, our know-how, our efficiency, and even our faith.

We are so sure of ourselves that we no longer

believe we must check our theories against the realities of life experienced by Fourth World families. But in fact these families ask for neither ideas nor dreams from us. They are not waiting to ponder with us over vast economic programmes. They want to understand why their income is never that of other families and how they are going to buy their children book bags and t-shirts. They want to know how to break the cycle of chronic unemployment and how their children will get proper education at school. "What can we do so our family will be respected and so our children will learn something in class? . . . How will they get through school and learn a trade? . . . How will my husband find a job, how shall we find a decent place to live?" The families constantly oblige us to face these basic issues. Not because they are narrow-minded but because experience has taught them that ideas may be valid for others but that all theories fail in the face of their extreme poverty. The very poorest represent the Achilles' heel of our finely-spun theories. And they are blessed, the architects of the new world, precisely because they relentlessly ask the essential questions: What is your justice, your democracy, your respect of life and family, your love of God really worth? How far do they reach, where are their limits? They are the blessed, provided we allow them to question us. Provided we do not refuse to be inconvenienced, made uncertain, losing prestige as we are bound to do. We shall have to cease barricading ourselves behind the cogency of our concepts.

This is the basic prerequisite. Unless we cast off our notions of superiority, the poor cannot count on us for their liberation. We shall moreover be preventing less educated and more humble people from joining them. Christ's lamentation on the Pharisees who prevent the poor from entering the Kingdom concerns us even more than we may suspect. By making our logic prevail, we also prevent simple, well-meaning people from reaching out to the poorest. Many would have been ready to meet fellow human beings, not to give alms and practise charity, but simply to journey a while with them and learn about life together. They are unpretentious people who do not consider themselves particularly effective. They may not deny the importance of organisations, but they feel that the essential thing is to meet and respect people. Those who make a great show of their intelligence and reasoning, and even sell them for good money, discourage and humiliate these unpretentious people, disparaging their naïvety and passing them off as ignorant of humanity's great causes. The learned thus sit in judgment over the humble, paralysing others into inaction. Of all the well-to-do, these people perhaps pose the greatest threat to the poor and to simple people of goodwill. They oppose what the latter recognise in their heart of hearts because it flows from their life experiences, namely that humanity is not made for such judgments and divisions. Only God may separate the wheat from the chaff on Judgment Day. Who on this earth can claim to know who are the Father's blessed, unless it be the poor and excluded? And who shall be the blessed, if not those who try to set them free by serving them, rather than by teaching them lessons? But to learn to serve, we must be personally available to the most downtrodden.

> *"If anyone comes to me*
> *and does not prefer me to his mother and father,*
> *his wife and children, his brothers and sisters—*
> *yes, even his own life—he cannot be my*
>   *disciple. . . .*
> *In the same way, any of you*
> *who does not give up everything*
> *cannot be my disciple."*

(Luke 14, 26-28 and 33-34)

Christ asked the poor to remain divested of worldly possessions, close to the excluded and capable of helping them break free of their shackles. He asked the well-to-do to guarantee the success of this endeavour by participating in it. To do so, they will become like the poor, and even smaller than the poor, truly poor in spirit and shedding real tears because the existence of the most exhausted truly makes them suffer.

This appeal has no relation with what we might consider an unhealthy attraction to living in misery. Neither does Jesus suggest we punish ourselves, using poverty and exile as a penance. Jesus is as realistic as are the poor. He knows their need and recognises their right to find others at their side who prove that fidelity to the rejected is possible. Others who say, "If I can be true, you can be even better." Otherwise, telling the poor they are blessed would be still another way of abandoning them to impossible tasks which the well-off are unwilling to undertake. Indeed, what would it mean to proclaim the inhabitants of a working-class neighbourhood capable of setting free the families of a nearby emergency housing settlement, if we ourselves would not restitute honour to these most deprived by sharing our lives with them? If we do not, we mock both the poor and the wretched.

To me, the Gospel has an awesome consistency and an unfailing realism. The Gospel not only recognises all human beings, but truly knows them. They are known in an unbearable and even pitiless way, as the love of God for all is constantly recalled. "When you give a banquet, do not invite your friends, brothers or sisters, or your rich neighbours. But when you give a banquet, invite the poor, the crippled, the lame, the blind, and you will be blessed. You will be repaid at the resurrection of the righteous." (Luke 14, 12-13) To Christ, banquets for the crippled were no manner of speech. Neither had they anything to do with our present-day systems of social benefits and public assistance to the poor. These systems no doubt have their value and should not disappear. But a Christian's business is elsewhere. The banquet Christ has in mind is not a form of aid, but a sharing of honour. It is also an extravagance: you, the crippled, are blessed; I will wash your feet and serve you at the table.

It is the extravagance of Zachea, a rich tax-collector who does not hesitate to climb a sycamore to get a glimpse of Jesus. He does not even try to speak to Him. He simply wants to catch sight of Him. Deeply moved and full of joy when the Lord asks for his hospitality, he decides to give half his fortune to the poor. The other half will serve to return fourfold the money unjustly extorted from his fellow men. The onlookers feel he exaggerates and Christ will have to explain to them, "Today, salvation has come to this house." (Luke 19, 9) Zachea will be the only rich man to receive this personal assurance of salvation from Jesus. By divesting himself of his possessions, he will have overturned the system of exploitation and economic abuse, which leads to total exclusion of the poorest. He will be criticised for it. Nor is there anything abstract in Christ's warning, "They will persecute you... You will be betrayed even by your parents... All others will hate you because of Me." (Luke 21, 12-19) The well-off who will follow in the footsteps of Zachea will deeply disturb the social, economic and religious order. They will not be appreciated for ceasing to bar the poor from the Kingdom. Christ honours them by offering them so difficult and necessary a mission.

For the poor not only need constant reminding of their role, they must also receive the means to assume it. Discovering and bringing forth these means are among the duties of the affluent. First, they must learn from the poor the nature and form of what is needed. What are their priorities? How can they be pursued? We cannot know offhand, since we have for so long dictated our own views to them, arrogating to ourselves the right to define their needs.

With Fourth World families in our own countries and overseas, we really must learn to stand in the back row. Those who are closest to them understand far better than we do what kind of education, vocational training, employment, unionising, housing, environment and cultural resources can best sustain them. We know nothing about these things in our own countries. We do not know what means are really needed for the hungry in Africa. We do not even know how to help them feed themselves or keep alive. Only our estimates of the bushels to be shipped to them may be reasonably accurate, and even here we may be mistaken. We know little about the state of bodies and minds among the very poorest people throughout the world. We make do with dubious approximations and stereotypes. We know nothing about how they search for their souls, unless we be among those missionaries so rarely listened to, among those far away priests who go unnoticed and forgotten by most of us. All we have learned about justice and the Kingdom, about democracy and human rights, we may have to unlearn to discover them anew. We can have no more reprimands in store for other citizens nor for governments, certainly not on the score of human rights violations. We do not even know what kind of legal assistance to offer to Fourth World families in our own cities and villages.

The role of the leader and teacher of course is scarcely compatible with that of the wise who must discover what is revealed off-hand to the humble. The leader can continue to pursue his personal well-being, his need to hoard security and honours. He can even pretend to be piling them up in order to redistribute them to the benefit of others. If, instead of being the master, he becomes the servant, his only concern will be to amass riches for his master. It must be one thing or the other. We cannot imagine bringing the Good News to the poor during our spare time, leading in fact an existence from which they are entirely absent. Neither can we think of devoting one or two years of our lives to them, and then run to catch up on lost time, to carry off a personal career. The poor and the rejected will not refuse such initiatives, but they will never consider them convincing. And with unconvincing Christians, they will not dare undertake a struggle to free themselves.

"I have come to set a fire on earth and how I wish it were already alight!" (Luke 12, 49) It is not with our lukewarm preferences, carefully calibrated solidarities and cool superiority that we shall kindle fires, nor sustain the fire lit by the Saviour. Jesus in extreme poverty truly represents a passion to share—and we cannot share passion as we might material possessions. "Where your treasure is, there too is your heart," Christ says. Decide what is your real treasure. There too will be your passion. Let us not claim to be cleverer than others, capable of a reasonable compromise, serving the poor on the one hand, and Mammon on the other, non-violence one moment and violence the next. We shall always try to do so anyway, because it is too difficult to part with our possessions without ever going back on such a renunciation. I am terrified at the thought of certain populations exhausted by extreme poverty, and whom militants set out to liberate. I see them kept in ignorance, manipulated in the name of their own best interests, treated as pawns even by their liberators. Some of them do so in the name of order, others in the name of a revolution. In either case, their action contradicts the Gospel, the Beatitudes and the Last Judgment.

The offer Jesus made the rich was also unconditional. Let us imagine what it meant to visit prisons, to enter the sheer hell of these places of impurity where prisoners were locked up with their guards. Let us think of what it meant to visit the lepers, to feed the impure and the cursed. It was a sure way of giving up one's status as son of a pure family, one's ascendancy which proved one's rights to honours and a respectable profession. Touching the impure, one would no longer be allowed to practise a pure profession. I feel that Christ's offer is equally unconditional today. It is difficult to maintain one's security, prestige, professional and social status when one moves into a dilapidated settlement, wedged between a canal and a highway, to become one with its inhabitants. Merely to support the idea of such a step and defend it before others already involves loss of prestige. He who does so no longer finds the establishment nor the revolution on his side. He thought he was of the world and he is no more.

I remember the cruel situation imposed on a priest who had joined an ATD Fourth World team in a particularly desolate shantytown north of Paris. In the nearby working-class parish, many reproved and discouraged him. To them, he had chosen the wrong way of fighting for the poor. It would create a most regrettable division within the general struggle of the workers. The priest felt he could cope with rats and cockroaches in his shantytown shack. He courageously endured the daily misfortunes he shared with the families. But he suffered bitterly being misunderstood by those who should have been closest to him and hearing his love for the poorest disparaged in parish meetings. I do not know if he ever got over it.

Exiled from his own milieu and forsaken by it, he who leaves his kin and friends will moreover not even have the consolation of finding the poor immediately on his side. He will have to live among them as an expatriate. He will no longer see familiar things and faces, walk no longer through familiar streets. And there where he has taken up residence, he knows neither the language, nor the mentality. It took unusual conviction to follow Jesus Christ to the bitter end in His own day and it takes just as much conviction now. We should be bent on arming and organizing ourselves in order to sustain one another so much more than we do. We should take the means to stand together side by side within the Church. The fate of the poorest and that of the whole Kingdom is at stake and yet we sometimes seem so little concerned. We do so little to organise ourselves for common training and action in the name of the Church and the people of God.

We have no alternative but to support one another if we want some chance of success and especially if we want to offer others the chance to be among the blessed of the Father. None of us can claim to make progress alone. Struggling by ourselves contradicts the Gospel. The truth can be held only *in common*, experienced together around Christ. And the truth is that if the rich do not share their possessions, love, intelligence and lives in unison, then the poor, the wretched and the rich will never unite to build a world of justice and brotherhood. All will go their separate ways. The poor will eventually be set free, as convenience allows. And the wretched will never be liberated at all.

I well realise all the opposition reared up against the very idea that rich and poor could unite. Misgivings are legitimate. Will the poor not pay once more for an alliance by submitting? The danger is real and we must be aware of it. But on the other hand we cannot ignore the danger that by failing to unite, even people of good will could end up by being at war with one another. They often live in mutual distrust which at times degenerates into hate. Yet, all seemed to want the same liberation at the outset. This way the very people who wanted justice cause the Kingdom to fail. A letter reminded me of this recently. It was sent to me by a family union, castigating me for having founded, with very poor families, an organisation in which better-off families can join them and support their struggle. The letter was harsh, and there we were, with no possibility left to work together.

By refusing to see people unite or by wanting to impose unity by force, do we not drive the rich to close themselves off more and more on their own intellectual, financial or religious campus? They will be tempted to turn it even more into the world's centre of gravity. This is how many movements begin marching without the poor in the front ranks. In many struggles for peace or liberty, the poor hold no leading part. God can change the hearts of the wealthy; God can do all, Christ says. What if we let Him do it? What if we help the Church? The Church's mission is not to do works of justice, but to *be* itself a work of justice and therefore of unity. In whose name would we prevent her from being that? By virtue of what kind of justice would we leave the rich aside, their minds forever beclouded by their possessions, forcing the poor to wage sad, impossible struggles alone? By what right would some people imagine they are more worthy than others to love their fellow human beings?

The Catholic Action Movement, it is true, taught us how people should strive for salvation through their social class. This represented a major step ahead, an important era in the advance of God's people. The Catholic Action helped us transcend the long-standing idea of personal salvation to be achieved by each on his own account. But today we can go further. The rich and the poor leading separate actions, with an obligatory division between workers on the one hand and management and intellectuals on the other—this can no longer satisfy us. In the long run, such a process is contradictory to the thirst for unity enshrined in all human hearts. It is alien to the very spirit of the Gospel. Even as is alien to the Gospel the present-day notion of "self-sufficiency" imposed—too. late—on developing countries. We now live in an age of *co-responsibility*. The poorest and their interpretation of the Gospel clearly tell us so. There are complementary roles to assume. Christians can no longer in good conscience tolerate discord between partners in God's overall plan for humanity.

If they did, they would admit that the Kingdom be closed to the rich. But with the road to unity blocked, what would be this Kingdom left to the poor? By forbidding some to enter, we close it to all. The time has come to shoulder fully our co-responsibility. The rich cannot go to Heaven alone and in their present state. They will enter with the poor, and allowing the poor to lead them. The poor will lead all others in. This is their honour, and such is God's plan.

To remain true to this plan, no doubt we are all in equal need of journeying through the Gospel. We need to see Jesus walking and sitting down in the midst of the crowd. We must feel His breath, hear Him talk with the excluded and with those around them. For all eternity, He placed Himself on the side of the parents whose children are taken into care and raised by others, on the side of the homeless families and of those who haunt the employment agencies to find work, on the side of men who stop at the pub to forget, or who lash out at their neighbours to work off the pain that overflows their hearts, to get rid of their hatred and be ready to love again. Christ is Himself the fire He wanted to kindle, loving His Father passionately and kindling passionate love all around Him. We must pray to Him constantly, in our homes and our churches. We must accept that our priests be with Him always, speaking of Him from the depths of their prayers. He alone can sustain the fire in us and within the Church. Provided we choose the paths where He walks, that we may meet His eyes, that we may meet the eyes of the leper, of the blind man He cured, of Mary Magdalene, and of Zachea who lost his head for joy.

The rich must rest assured that Christ's gaze is one of friendship and tenderness, never of hate.

"They have hurt me so much, they have taken my children from me. Yet I have forgiven everything." Hundreds of men and women in areas of extreme poverty have spoken to me this way. They also echo Christ's words on the Cross: "It is not their fault, really; how could they know what they were doing?" Those who speak this way are no heroes. They simply know that forgiving is part of their own survival. But they are waiting for Christians to come tell them, "Your forgiveness is the forgiveness of God. All humanity needs your forgiveness, for it is founding the Kingdom."

All the rich, all Christians will not go to bring the Good News into poverty areas and share people's lives there. Much else remains to be done. Doors must be opened in the world around us, institutions must prepare to welcome the poor, structures must change. To achieve all this, hearts must be changed. The very poor are exacting masters. They show us the full measure of our responsibilities. These are manifold and demanding: changing the schools, our hospitals, the functioning of our democracy. And preparing our parishes, our communities, our diocesan bodies, so that they may form all at once a Church going out to the Fourth World, through its envoys and its nuns, and a Church awaiting its guests at the feast. If these Christians are not Christ Himself in the Fourth World, then who will be? If Christians do not convey to the families the passion of the Kingdom they long for, then who will? Who will venture into unknown slums, to remote poverty-stricken city outskirts, to the hamlets in some forgotten bush, where bodies and minds waste away? And who will set the table and await the guests at the feast? Who will prepare the rejoicing, if not the Christians? We are bound to do so, not because we are better than others, but because this is the mission Christ gave us.

But then what profound change in ourselves, what overwhelming stir in our institutions awaits us! What deep-cutting modifications in our ways of looking at the poor! They will cease to be recipients who depend on our charities, duly registered and accounted for at the entrance. Their relations with us will be radically different as they become our partners, and our teachers, while we are the ones who solicit their counsel and trust. What joy, but also what upheaval, when we shall find ourselves fully of the Church because the poor will have taught us at last that the first human right and the one which crowns all others is the right to spirituality! We can allow the poorest to fulfil all their aspirations and dreams, drawing their strength from God, on the condition that not only our hearts but also our organisations vouch for them and change accordingly. If we launch our dreams so high that the Utopia of a new world becomes a reality within the Church, this may modify much in our Catholic action, our Catholic schools and universities, our "grass-roots communities," our search for new forms of consecrated life. The poorest as ourselves, their pains our own pains, their expectations, joy and exultation our own—what changes for us and for the whole world!

Like the new-born who changes everything between husband and wife and in the family, the very poor transform everything when returning to the churches where they dared come no longer. Nothing will be as it was, not because of a new liturgy, but because people's hearts, be they rich or poor, will have changed, Jesus Christ being known and loved in the most wretched among them.

A friend of mine is a retired general. One day he came into contact with the ATD Fourth World Movement, and he began wishing to serve very poor families. He accepted office work, compiled dossiers, set out to defend requests in ministries. Eventually, he took charge of relations with the French National Assembly. He made every effort to have a Fourth World inter-party group established in the chamber. Thanks to him, the term "Fourth World" was pronounced before that body for the first time, in 1978. He then extended his efforts to the French Senate, while his idea for an inter-party group on extreme poverty was also gaining ground in the European Parliament. My friend rarely took the floor in meetings, and he did not write books. He had no liking for theories on poverty. A man of authority had made himself a servant, and divested of all personal ambition, his actions unknown by most, he became the silent artisan of a truly new process in European democracies. Members of Parliament started to commit themselves to the poorest.

Mr. Philippe Gouraud did not leave his Paris apartment. I do not know what has changed in his personal life, for he is not a man to indulge in confidences. But I imagine, having witnessed these things again and again, what compromising himself with Fourth World families may have cost him in family ties and social relations. Having chosen new priorities which he could not hide from his entourage he must at times feel like an outsider, having become a different man within the milieu where he had been at home all his life. His is a silent, unostentatious expatriation. Many of my friends experience it, enduring the disparaging comments, the quirked eyebrows, the inevitable humiliations when in the family circle or at official dinner parties they bring up the Fourth World. My friend Gouraud had certainly never thought himself to be blessed by the Father. Until the day, no doubt, when a Fourth World volunteer said to him: "Don't you understand? The blessed of the Father, that's you!" He was surprised. He loved God, he loved the poorest, he did not give much thought to himself. Many friends of mine among the better-off seem to have this in common. They do not ask themselves what their place is or whether they have a place. They are far too busy developing their action and service. They worry about the benefits the families may draw from them. They will reach Judgment Day, profoundly surprised to learn that by becoming new people, vulnerable, compromised and compromising, they were joining the just, the partners Jesus awaited.

I believe the situation of such men and women who remain in their own milieu may become difficult, and even untenable at times. For they are bound to make their entourage see itself for what it really is. People around will not be grateful for this. It must not have been easy for Nicodemus to "come into the light" and make manifest the works of God in an environment that did its utmost to keep disturbing truths at bay. For some of my friends, it would have been easier to leave all behind, if having a family to care for had not prevented them. When observing their painfully steady progress, I wonder how we can imagine that Christ could have loved the poor against the rich. He loved the poor *for* the rich. He loved Zachea for the poor and the exploited. He loved Nicodemus who still had progress to make. He loved the rich to the point of wanting them, at whatever cost, to be the blessed of the Father.

CHAPTER TWELVE

Saint Joseph, the Believer of All Times

The salvation of the poorest, the participation of the poor in the establishment of the Kingdom, the benediction of the wealthy who renounce their privileges. . . . Where did this incredible story begin? How did it become part of the history of humanity, transforming it from end to end? Joseph and Mary together formed the gateway through which Jesus entered humanity. A man and a woman, the first poor people the Gospel presents to us: what do we know of them? They founded the Holy Family, receiving, raising and educating Jesus. They remain forever the model, the ideal for all families. But how do we actually see them in the Gospel? To conclude this book, let us linger a while with them.

Why did I choose to place Joseph and Mary at the end, rather than at the beginning of this peregrination through the Gospel? In fact, I never felt capable myself of imagining these immeasurable personalities before having followed and meditated at length on the Messiah whom they offered to the world. The adult life of Christ tells me much about their lives and identities. I approach them differently after having seen Jesus among the crowd, touching the eyes of a blind man, multiplying the loaves or arguing in the synagogue. The Mother of God and the Holy Family will always remain a mystery. But I lived a good part of my existence at a time when it was not customary to contemplate and be filled with wonder by them. The Holy Family had but a modest place in most Christians' thinking, the family as such was not a focus of their attention. Joseph was remembered first and foremost as a worker. A somewhat narrow picture, when it comes to accounting for the gift of the Jewish people to humanity. Don't we need a broader understanding of the personalities emerging from its very depths, chosen by God to receive His only Son? The families in extreme poverty who could not allow themselves to lose their sense of family—their last defence against the world's cruelty—infallibly led me to a deeper view of the Holy Family. So did, most forcefully, Christ forsaken, Christ the Saviour of a people in poverty. The oppressed of today and of the past helped me imagine a greater and more exalting mystery. When I looked at the adult Jesus, the personalities of His parents took on more distinctive traits, a new splendour, an increasingly impressive depth. Jesus, and those who

243

constantly surround Him and whom He loves today as He did yesterday, have enlightened me. So I now return to Joseph and Mary, understanding better how they came to stand there as the doorway through which Jesus entered the history of humanity. It reassures me to know that they are forever encamped in the heart of the world.

Let me first speak about Joseph of whom the Gospel discloses so little. This seems to have allowed us to make more or less of him at different times. Apparently, the Gospel leaves us a certain liberty of interpretation. We use it to embellish or diminish his image to suit our taste. Some Christians even seem to manipulate or exploit him according to their whims. In this, Saint Joseph shares the lot of the poorest. He, more than many others in Christ's life, remains a witness to the changes of minds and hearts throughout the centuries. It is not by mere chance that today we stylise him, presenting him as a symbol rather than as a living person whom we should meet face to face. In as much as he takes a more human shape, he does so as a manual worker or as a craftsman. In this way, we obscure the true story of this man of the House of David; we obliterate his essential dimensions and his crucial role. Isn't this a considerable loss?

Through our unwary interpretations, Joseph's personality is warped, blurred and lifeless. His fixed image can neither guide, inspire, nor amaze us. I wonder how we can love him. The Church tells us about him, without much encouraging us to walk with him, to let him surprise and jostle us. I fear that in the minds of many he has become a boneless silhouette, just a necessary touch to complete the background, rather than a character who stands in the limelight. Was his part in life really so unobtrusive, Joseph the symbol of obedience, the honest carpenter accepting without a murmur an outside intervention in his married life so that God's plan might follow its course? I cannot believe this. The crowds in the Gospel, the poorest around me, Christ Himself, all lead me to quite a different man.

"Then Joseph her husband, being a just man, and not willing to make her a public example, was minded to put her away quietly." (Matthew 1, 19) Comments on this text express surprise. What was meant by this secret repudiation never mentioned in the Old Testament? But is there real ground for such questioning? Saint Matthew insists that Joseph of the House of David was a righteous man. In other words, he was a man profoundly moulded by the scriptures and by Davidic tradition. He had his ideas about justice, be it God's justice or the law as doctors and scribes had developed it. A carpenter learned in the Word of God would not undergo unthinkingly his worldly condition nor be witness to the oppression inflicted upon his people of Galilee by the Romans and by its own wealthy. He certainly had precise ideas about justice, comparing the word and the acts of the Pharisees to the plan of God revealed in the holy books. He must have experienced the distortions and the incompatibilities in his own existence. Did he perhaps consider the public repudiation of a young woman pregnant out of wedlock to figure among these distortions? A man from the House of David, respected in theory as the son of one of the "pure" families, he was in reality one of a people whose society and culture were left to collapse. A carpenter holding an honourable trade in theory, he was in reality the victim of the underemployment and poverty that had broken in on the people of Galilee. Would this not have given Joseph much food for thought regarding the justice of man and of God? At least to the eyes of the poor, it seems highly improbable that he would not have had personal ideas. The opposite would have meant that he was a weak man, without character. Would such a man have been chosen to be the father and educator of Jesus? I am convinced, as are Fourth World families, that the image of Joseph as a just man is meant to be taken literally, precisely because he was all at once a man of God and profoundly marked by the oppression exerted by human beings. "I bet he had a lot to say about all that!", as a man put it after listening to the reading of the Gospel on Christmas Eve.

Joseph, a man of conviction, of personal ideas, who compared the realities of his day to the Scriptures and found them unbearable, Joseph, following in the steps of his Davidic ancestors—such was the first vision the Fourth World gave me of him. If Jesus was so familiar with the Pharisees without being one of them, if He was so aware of their errors and hypocrisies, no doubt it was His divinity that revealed to Him all that people tended to conceal. But I cannot fail to also credit Joseph, who attended to Christ's early education. Jesus grew up in a home where He heard His father decry the Pharisees. No doubt, it was from Joseph that He first heard it said that the Pharisees barred the access of the poor to God. I feel certain that this must have been a much discussed subject at the home of Joseph and Mary. I can hear Joseph holding forth on this heated topic of the day. I have no reason to imagine him taciturn. Jesus certainly did not acquire His first concerns nor learn His first prayers from a silent man, beset by dreams only at night.

Joseph has his place among the just, beside Mary but also beside Simeon, Anne and Zacharias. They all knew one another in those days and I fail to see why Joseph should be considered a mere figurehead, just good enough to be his wife's husband. It would be a way of degrading not only God's plan for the world but also His mysterious alliance with the Jewish people for all time.

I have already insisted upon the disrespect for God which consists of presenting Him as a mere producer, setting up situations for the sake of demonstration. He would not make little of the liberation of the poor, reducing it to an incidental act, unsupported by history and running parallel to it. God *is* the liberation of the poor, He enters into their history on earth, which is an essential and enlightening part of the history of all humanity. A "liberation theology" that would ignore this would make no sense. It could not be a theology in the eyes of the Church. Similarly, if God only cast actors, He would not be God. He would intervene outside history, whereas He, in fact, is part of history. God needs no artificial backdrops and Joseph was not part of a backdrop. God's setting is the world's history and Joseph was a man of his time, a righteous man such as the history of the Jewish people made them.

If we ignore this, we also forget God's alliance with the Jewish people, a permanent alliance in which God walks with the Jews and, through them, with all humanity. Joseph of the House of David could welcome the Saviour because like Anne, Simeon and Zacharias, he awaited a Saviour. God spoke to him only in his dreams. Do we realise what that tells us about the man he was? A man of prayer, totally kneaded by the reality of God. God does not speak this way to dreamers but to men and women who constantly question Him, in order to act according to His will. Joseph is such a man and his responses therefore are immediate. He never hesitates. What God required of him, he was already expecting.

I suppose that Joseph, like Mary, like the Zealots and many others, prayed ardently for a Messiah who would cause the mighty to renounce their thrones and cease dominating the humble. In the manner of his days, surely he was waiting for the Messiah to bring this internal Kingdom where all would find their full identity as children of God. Let us consider what he saw happening under his own eyes, the systematic impoverishment of his people, the spoliation of their communal land and, thereby, the breakdown of the community and its system of mutual aid. The large estates replacing the ancestral fields, the usurers bleeding dry the peasants who could not pay their taxes, no protection left to women, widows, orphans and the poor. . . . Could Joseph as a just man who loved God accept such iniquity?

Could he accept the further injustice caused by the haughtiness and arrogance of those who held high rank at the Temple in Jerusalem, oppressing growing numbers of poor who were unable to pay the tithes or conform with the rites? I think Joseph fervently waited for a Saviour to liberate his people from the Romans, but also from all sin, from all unfaithfulness to God. No doubt, he readily accepted a life of sobriety, but he also hoped for justice, fraternity and truth.

I imagine that, being of the House of David, Joseph must have heard about the coming of the Messiah since his early childhood. It was certainly customary in the families descended from the Patriarchs to pass down the Messianic calling from one generation to another. Joseph always appears to me in his identity as the son of one of these families. His own father must have spoken as did his ancestors. He, in turn, will pass on the heritage to Jesus. Mary's Magnificat must have resounded in Joseph too, and its vision and language are going to become familiar to Jesus. Later, Christ will carry with Him the words so often heard: "The Lord makes blind the mighty and conceals from them what He reveals to the small; He overturns their thrones and lifts up the humble." The application of this prophecy by Christ Himself will surpass and even overturn anything Joseph had ever imagined. Yet he has the foreknowledge handed down from the depth of his people's memory. Christ in realising the plan of God did not come as a punishment to the Jewish people, but as the reward for their long and faithful waiting. He did not come as a burden entrusted to Joseph, but as the reward for the righteous man who had waited with trust.

If so, the birth of Jesus in a Davidic family was in no way a mere formality. Joseph was not there only so that this birth could be formally registered. As a man both of his time and deeply rooted in history, he received Jesus into his family to take full responsibility for His education. Could we think for a single moment that he would not have done so with care and conviction? Is it imaginable that he would not have actively undertaken to form the child Jesus' intelligence and heart? He certainly did so all the more fervently, as he saw himself and his people threatened by disintegration. He, the carpenter, must have had the time for this and ample reasons to reflect, while waiting for orders that became more and more rare. He must also have had urgent motivations for strengthening his son in the ways of God's justice, at a time when traditions weakened.

We cannot be surprised then that Jesus had such extraordinary knowledge of the Scriptures. No doubt God gave Him the comprehension, but He was also constantly taught by Joseph. His explanations of the texts were of course divinely inspired. But they also were clearly the readings of a man in poverty confronted with the basic realities of everyday life. Would not the experience and teachings of Joseph have played a role in this? Much of what Jesus said to the priests at the synagogue could have been said by the carpenter comparing the works and words of the learned and the Pharisees to the teachings of the Prophets.

I have known many craftsmen: saddlers, blacksmiths,

tanners, carpenters, born into rural crafts and who sank into extreme poverty as their communities frayed. I remember Mr. Bonnavo, one of the wise men among the families of the Camp at Noisy-le-Grand. He used to cite the word of God when expressing his disapproval of the ever-increasing rejection of the poorest. His mother, the wife of a saddler's assistant, had taught him the Gospel along with the alphabet. But he had never gone further than working as an apprentice with his own father, a jobbing workman himself. One day the craftsman who employed them went out of business; their trade was dying. Mr. Bonnavo never complained about his material deprivation, though his family did not always eat to its heart's content. But he complained about the harshness of people, about their contempt for fellow human beings overcome by misery.

There must have been many similar people around Joseph in Galilee before the census ordered by Augustus Caesar. Even if Joseph was still at work, he must have been very poor because he certainly shared the fruits of his labour with those even more rarely employed than he. No wonder he appeared at the inn at Bethlehem after a long journey as a man to be sent on to a cave. Why would the innkeeper have thought of this? I see Joseph arriving there, frayed and exhausted, certainly not the only one to be referred to such an emergency shelter. At the time, a great number of extremely poor families seem to have dwelt in such makeshift homes in the hills.

But through the eyes of Fourth World families, I see foremost an active and thoughtful man who evolves over time. A man experiencing the realities of his day, living a destiny true to the history of his people and learning from it. A man who never ceases to progress and strengthen his personality. Joseph betrothed to Mary is not yet Joseph arriving in Bethlehem, with Jesus just about to be born. And the Joseph of Bethlehem still has a long road before him, passing through exile as did his ancestors, be they refugees or deported. As a refugee in Egypt where he could not work except in forced labour or as a slave, Joseph will relive and epitomise the destiny of his entire people. And like any father, he gains maturity as a man and as a father while Jesus grows up. Of these years of maturing, the Gospel does not speak. This should be no reason not to meditate on them. Should not the silence of the Gospel at least lead us to silent contemplation, to seeking deeper understanding? I cannot do otherwise when facing the man who guided the first steps, thoughts and prayers of the infant Jesus. It is Joseph who later provides the adolescent Jesus with a vocabulary, teaches Him a mode of thought, opens to Him an environment in which to train His sensitivity. I feel certain that the life, the personality and the heart of Joseph were exactly right for introducing Jesus among humanity. How then would we not yearn to know him better?

As for me, the Gospel's silence about the years in Egypt fills me with terror. What were they like, these years of wandering, of solitude no doubt, and of humiliations worse than those experienced in Galilee and Judea? Did the family go hungry? Did they keep company with other wretched people? What work did Joseph find? With no facts, we can only imagine their desperate situation and meditate in silence, awestruck by this Holy Family in flight.

"When they had gone,
an angel of the Lord appeared to Joseph in a dream.
"Get up," he said. "Take the child
and His mother and escape to Egypt.
Stay there until I tell you,
for Herod is going to search for the child
to kill Him."
So he got up,
took the child and His mother during the night
and left for Egypt,
where he stayed until the death of Herod.
And so was fulfilled what the Lord had said
through the prophet: 'Out of Egypt I called my
     Son'."

(Matthew 2, 13-15)

Matthew either tells us too much or too little. For all this cannot have happened without agitation. "Herod is going to search for the child to kill Him", what horrifying news! What frantic efforts to assemble the essentials quickly, rush to the road and reach the desert where the soldiers will not pursue them! After that, we have no more images. What did the eyes of the infant Jesus see? What sounds did His ears make out? What were the loneliness, the anxiety, but also the courage and hope of Joseph and Mary? In our ignorance, what else can we do but meditate and grope for understanding through constant prayer?

By the time they could return to their land, Joseph must have matured considerably, his convictions even firmer, his hope more ardent. The fire that Jesus Christ later wanted to kindle in the world, would He not as an adolescent have sensed it in His father's heart? Had Joseph not given the example of the love of God burning as a fire in men's and women's hearts? For Joseph will still need to love God fervently, in order to take up life in Nazareth again. No doubt his place as a carpenter has been taken, the ever fewer customers of old having turned to others. And Joseph will have to get accustomed again to the lies, suspicion, denunciation, domination which have permeated more than ever the communities of Galilee, weighing heavily on the poor and the poorest. His Jewish people who disfigure themselves by disfiguring the poor, Joseph will have to love deeply and to fervently love God, in order to take up his old existence, to travel to Jerusalem again, year after year, to celebrate Passover. It means much more than just picking up old habits. Joseph must virtually remarry his people and their history, so as to truly integrate Jesus. At least this is what I learn in Saint Luke's account of Christ's first words at the Temple. No matter how disappointed or discouraged, Joseph never forgot God nor the mission he had been given to accept as a son He who would deliver the people from sin.

Jesus certainly went too quickly in the eyes of His father. What was He doing there, sitting in the midst of the Temple teachers, listening and even talking to them? He is much too young and this is not the conduct Joseph considers fit for the Saviour. He is baffled. "Son, why have you treated us like this? Your father and I have been anxiously searching for you." (Luke 2, 48) This anxiety for the Messiah, the bewilderment about God's plan for Him were certainly not new to His parents. The terrible threat of Herod, the massacre of the innocents, the weary exile in Egypt, the return to Nazareth where people's relationships are poisoned by injustice and contempt . . . , Joseph must have often questioned God on this manner of protecting and preparing the Saviour. God seems to have spoken to him no more after his return to Galilee where the commandments are heeded even less than before. Has he been mistaken? He thought he was serving the Lord. Perhaps it was all an illusion? "'Why were you searching for me?' Jesus asked. 'Didn't you know I had to be in my Father's house?' But they did not understand what He was saying to them." (Luke 2, 49-50) When contemplating Joseph in Nazareth, I feel I am in the presence of a just and strong man who fulfils his responsibilities without swerving but who also fights with God: "I do that which You have asked of me, Lord, but what do You do to achieve man's salvation?"

Did God put an early end to this struggle by calling Joseph to Him? I have often asked myself why we suppose him to be dead by the time Jesus began His public life. We have no certainty, no clear indications in this regard and by abbreviating his life, we also cut off the meditation on a man who might still have much to tell us. Did we feel it was necessary that

Mary be widowed at an early age to guarantee her virginity? I do not know. But unless we can ascertain the fact, declaring Joseph prematurely dead may not be wise. If Jesus had been an orphan when He was thirty, would they have said of Him in Nazareth, "Is He not the carpenter's son?" (Matthew 13, 55) If the carpenter had been dead, the people of Nazareth would have said, "Is this not the son of Joseph of the House of David?" In making Joseph die early, do we not risk bypassing an essential phase of his destiny which could teach and inspire us?

For my part, I often wonder what may have gone through Joseph's mind seeing his son depart to be swallowed by the crowd. "He was obedient to them. . . . Jesus grew in wisdom and stature, and in favour with God and with the people." (Luke 2, 51-52) Jesus had been a good son to Joseph and His father had raised Him to be a good servant, held in high esteem by God and the people. Now there He goes, not to the Temple to take His rightful place in the face of the mighty, but to the poor, the maimed, the wretched, the people of ill repute! What can He expect of them, what kind of liberation is this? He is heading for disaster, to be sure!

What terrifying surrender indeed to these destitute men and women with their broken bodies and discomposed faces, ignorance written all over them. For Joseph knows the poor and the poorest. He knows them all the better for having loved them all his life, as he would the innocent victims of the power of the wealthy. He has shared with them the little he had, even if it meant depriving himself. I feel sure Jesus sometimes had to go without a meal and miss out on basic necessities because of the generosity of His parents toward those in need. Let us think of what it meant to be a righteous man in Nazareth in those days of acute economic depression. I have known just men in all areas of extreme poverty throughout the world. They are forever on the move, trying to redress a wrong done to a neighbour, while their wives empty their own cupboards and give away the last bottle of milk, the last loaf of bread, so that another mother's children will not go hungry. Where misery prevails, righteous people have busy lives. The poorest are always on their doorsteps to ask for help, the most wretched are always around the next corner, innocently waiting for them to pass by. Their wives and children have but one choice: either they set themselves against too much generosity because it deprives them of what they need, or they join in their husband's or father's struggle. Mary and Jesus certainly did not set themselves against Joseph's sense of justice. Did not Joseph teach the child and the young man his own ever-deepening love for the poor who never left him in peace? But now he sees Jesus depart, not to reprimand the mighty who are unfaithful to God, but to convert the crowds! Could that not wait? The Prophets before Him never acted that way! He, who could have become a doctor of law, is going to lose all His prestige. "My son was so intelligent, honest and capable. He could rival any scribe, Pharisee or doctor. He had a brilliant future ahead of Him and there He goes and squanders it all!"

I have known many such anxious and disappointed

fathers. There was the father of Gabrielle, an ATD Fourth World volunteer. He had taught her everything: faith, integrity, respect for the poor. . . She had a good teaching career ahead of her. One day, she left to join the Camp of the Homeless at Noisy-le-Grand. She did so not even to carry out a precise professional project, but simply to share the existence, pain and hope of families submerged in mud, refuse and misery. If Gabrielle had committed herself to people of her own milieu or to the Red Cross or Caritas to assist the poor, her father would have been content. If she had taken the veil, he would have been happy and thanked God. But she was throwing in her lot with a population so wretched that it had broken adrift from all established institutions. She disregarded all the rules that govern action and relationships between the poor and the well-off; she overturned long-standing priorities. Gabrielle's father could not conceive of such a choice. He did not know and could not yet understand that this was how the radical change of hearts and customs desired by God must come about. He had told her himself about God who wants justice to rule the world. He certainly expected his daughter to follow in his footsteps as a righteous person and to do even more and better than he. One of his sons had become a Jesuit priest. It had made him infinitely proud. But Gabrielle was not doing more and better than her father. She was doing *otherwise*. And she did so with only a handful of companions recruited by an unknown priest who had no prestige, no power or influence. Her father could not understand and for years he did all he could to coax her home, to get her to marry or return to teaching. Finally he resigned himself but he never

258

admitted he had done so. His daughter had renounced all prestige, all financial but also all moral,
intellectual and religious securities. Even if he had to
accept this, he could never rejoice nor be reassured.
Only after his death did his family come across a
letter in which he said he congratulated himself for
having given two children to the Church: his son
Richard, the Jesuit, and his daughter Gabrielle.

The mystery of a father's heart, the mystery of
God's mercy... Such fathers of volunteers always
make me turn to Joseph. Volunteers are not Christ
and Joseph's heartbreak must have been a hundred-
fold that of these parents today. His son, as we said,
does not go to any of the places or groups that could
have served as stepping stones for His action as a
Saviour: the synagogues, the Pharisees, the Esseni-
ans, nor even the Zealots. (He had a wide choice
there, after all.) He leaves Nazareth, solitary and
poor as Job, to join the crowds. Joseph's son, the
Messiah, without a stone on which to lay His head
and provoke all established groups. He could at least
have made use of one of them, just as Gabrielle could
have joined Caritas or a religious community. But He
surrounds Himself instead with some humble fish-
ermen who follow Him, their hands as empty as His
own. Worse, He takes on a tax collector! Is He not
bound to fall into general disgrace?

Though a defender of the most vulnerable himself,
desirous all his life of seeing men establish ties of love
and equality worthy of the children of God, nothing
had really prepared Joseph to foresee the actual plan
of Christ. Yet of this plan he had been an essential

259

component: a righteous man, kneaded and formed by poverty, exclusion and misery, called to introduce Jesus into the world from the bottom. But as such, he was part of God's history in the world, without having the means to understand it. He could in no way believe that the Kingdom would come into the world from the poorest quarters. His culture had taught him that great restorations came from the top. The families liable to give birth to the Messiah, according to tradition, were well respected. Significant reconversion to God could be operated only by the intervention of people of learning, prestige and irreproachable conduct. Christ takes the opposite road, thereby signifying not necessarily His social, but His religious and cultural revolution. Jesus has deeply instilled in Him the teachings of Joseph, His heart and mind have been formed by constant contact with the poor and the wretched who flocked around His father. Yet He did not imitate Joseph.

Jesus took on the human condition, not to follow a human vision but to transform man's condition through and through from within. This meant transforming from within even the condition and mode of thought of Joseph. How could Joseph have understood? He truly believed he had accomplished all his duties toward the Messiah. Now he discovers that even his own views and convictions are questioned by the Saviour. He was actively participating in the world's salvation. And here he is called upon to convert himself with all the poor around him. Can this be serious or is he being held up to ridicule? Either Jesus is in error or he himself has been wrong all these years. Joseph himself called to conversion?

Joseph converting himself to this Jesus who ignores all the rules? Jesus is faithful to the Scriptures no doubt, but He is totally different from all the models and stereotypes the Jews have imagined in all good faith. And He has chosen a path that can lead nowhere. Joseph who understands the ways of the world cannot think otherwise. To fail in order to succeed, to succeed through failure is an idea as foreign to his culture as remaking the world beginning at the bottom. Can it be that he who has given so much for the salvation of humanity will never see it? "Whoever loves his father or his mother more than me is not deserving of me." To leave His father, to have to choose between His father and God. . . . What parent could have suffered more deeply from these words than Joseph?

Christ turned the world upside-down, even Joseph's world. And Joseph, despite his poverty, had remained a son of David, well versed in religious matters. His very learning now hinders his comprehension of the salvation brought about by the Messiah. Even he will not escape Christ's warning that the wise would not understand what would be revealed to the humble. Would this not have been the real upheaval in the life of Joseph? He, the man of justice, experience and wisdom, must forget all he learned, relearn all about salvation and the justice of God. I doubt that the revolution in his life came from the Lord's demand that he receive Jesus. That proposal was in keeping with the hopes of a descendant of David. I fall into silence before the older, more mature Joseph, his task accomplished, of whom, after so much fidelity, God still asks that he become converted.

I do not know if Joseph was still alive, but I feel he was. How could God not have let him complete his role even to the last heartbreak? There are no reasons to think that God would not have invited him to fulfil his destiny up to his ultimate conversion. I feel sure he was offered the chance—as had been Gabrielle's father—to convert himself to this Jesus whom he had loved, protected and educated so faithfully, only to find Him so far out of reach in the end. Joseph, as I see him, disappointed, bewildered, torn apart, awes me. How did his heart accept the truth in the end? I feel that Joseph, so sorely tried, walks ahead of us and of the whole Church. The believers, are they not he, throughout the ages, believing themselves saved and discovering they are not even converted yet? For who among us is truly converted to Jesus Christ, the most wretched of men, dying on the Cross between the penitent and the unrepentant thieves? Saint Joseph preceding us because—how could we doubt this?—as his task had come to an end, he accepted to begin all over again.

CHAPTER THIRTEEN

Magnificat!

Mary said,
"My heart praises the Lord;
my soul is glad because of God, my Saviour,
for He has remembered me, His lowly servant!
From now on all generations will call me blessed,
because of the great things
the Mighty God has done for me.
Holy is His name;
from one generation to another
He shows mercy to those who honour Him.
He has stretched out His mighty arm
and scattered the proud with all their plans.
He has brought down mighty kings from their
       thrones,

and lifted up the lowly.
He has filled the hungry with good things,
and sent the rich away with empty hands.
He has kept the promise He made to our ancestors
and has come to the help of His servant Israel.
He has remembered to show mercy to Abraham
and to all his descendants forever!"

(Luke 1, 46-55)

The Lord has come forth. He has scattered the proud and exalted the humble. Justice is accomplished. The Magnificat is the most resplendent of victory hymns. Such exultation does not spring from the lips of a shy and pious young girl who knows nothing of the world. Mary appears to us shining with trust in God and commitment to humanity. Betrothed to Joseph, she belongs to one of these families which often bring forth just people. Pure families, passing down the Scriptures from generation to generation, but without wealth and close to the poor, as were the Patriarchs. These families, nurtured on the Prophets, were the cradle of men and women of integrity, but also of strength and energy, for they led a frugal and rough existence. Mary was one of them. Unless her Magnificat be considered a literary exercise or the sole fruit of divine inspiration, we must take it to express an extraordinary will to participate in the plan of God.

Even as Joseph, Mary shows this unfaltering will straight away by her reply to the Angel: "Behold the handmaid of the Lord, be it done unto me according to thy word." Mary was a servant, not yet in the sense which Christ would embody, but a servant according to the tradition of her people, a woman serving God in righteousness, actively accomplishing His works. She is the perfect woman of the Scriptures, depicted in the Proverbs:

> *How hard it is to find a capable wife! . . .*
> *She gets up before daylight*
> *to prepare food for her family*
> *and to tell her servant girls what to do.*
> *She looks at land and buys it,*
> *and with money she has earned she plants a*
> *   vineyard.*
> *She is a hard worker, strong and industrious.*
> *She knows the value of everything she makes,*
> *and works late into the night.*
> *She is generous to the poor and needy. . . .*
> *Her husband is well-known, one of the leading*
> *   citizens.*

(Proverbs 31, 10-23)

Women of the era of electronics in our own part of the world would say that this perfect woman toiled hard at countless domestic tasks. Yet she held a more important social and economic role than her sisters among us do today, even if they have jobs outside the home. Even when she had no servants, she was the one who presided over the family budget and controlled the quality of goods. She could secure an independent revenue, have a voice in family and community affairs, and directly create justice, for it was she who decided what should be shared with the poor.

By choosing Mary, God chose the perfect woman, proud and ready to assume full responsibility for her mission. When meditating on her, I always think of the disconcerting social climate that virtually enfolds her and molds her from early childhood on. The social climate of Galilee cut adrift, people clinging to traditions no longer in tune with everyday life. People on whom the Temple no longer relies and who can rely on no one. Before them always loom the religious authorities, the guardians of the Law, intent on maintaining customs and rites, often pitiless and all the more bent on regulating people's lives as they can no longer control them. Behind them stand Herod and the Romans, equally iniquitous. Mary is raised under these harsh conditions and molded by them as she grows up. She is a woman well-informed of her people's turmoils, and one who travels, be it only to Jerusalem each year for Passover.

Perfect, active and poor, Mary consciously takes part in Galilean history, as much as does Joseph, or even more. The men carry the ritual alms to the synagogue; the women take charge of practical sharing on their doorstep. They serve food in their courtyards, offer clothing and blankets. They "put out their hands," as the Proverbs say. They meet the poor and the wretched face to face, they touch them, care for them, they are personally involved. This has been the pattern worldwide, and this personal, direct role of women in regard to the unfortunate continues in many parts. Only women in rich countries no longer meet the poor and the poorest. Elsewhere, the poor meet women much more often than they do men, and the women really know them. I see Mary even more involved than Joseph, touching more directly the misery which spreads around her. While walking among the crippled and the famished, she must have felt with her whole being that, without justice, love cannot exist, and without love, justice is hollow for the poor.

In this daily struggle which she fully assumed, she needed all the more courage. As a young Jewish woman of a poor, rural community, she knew what to expect if she gave birth to an illegitimate child. Even if she could trust Joseph, motherhood under the circumstances would be difficult. But to crown all, she would mother the Son of God, heir to the throne of David. Mary knows her people's history. The Jews were not in the habit of welcoming their own prophets. The just who were awaiting the Saviour could not hope that He would be received in peace. The mighty would have to renounce their thrones, and Mary knew these people whose doctrines were but "commandments of men." (Matthew 15, 1-9) "Hypocrites . . . transgressing the commandment of God by virtue of their traditions," they were not ready to surrender. In the meantime, what would become of her child?

Mary went ahead, her eyes wide open. She would be defenceless before the hardships and sufferings awaiting her unless God will protect her. She must confide in Him for the realisation of His plan, but also for the daily security of the family she was going to found. She could no longer rely on her own strength as she had before. If she accepted what was announced to her, praising God with all her soul, it was because she now drew all her strength from Him.

She must also have had that stubbornness of the poor which stems from their very condition. For when poverty is injustice, it breeds obstinacy. I have lived all my life among obstinate families. They barricaded themselves behind their refusal to accept indignity and injustice, to the point of closing themselves off and "going their own way," as civil servants would put it. Mary certainly had the strength not to shut herself up, and I see her all the more headstrong and stubborn. To take on her task, she must have been the Queen of Courage. Otherwise, life would have defeated her.

This is how Mary appears to the families who experience misery. My own mother saw her this way. She measured the Holy Virgin's courage by the wilfulness she had to display herself to keep her children from being taken from her and to raise them in awe of God. This alone was difficult. Also, my mother was an obstinate woman. And she turned to the Virgin in full confidence. Mary could understand her plight since she had suffered, dared and achieved so much more. My mother also pitied her, picturing her pains, her humiliations and disappointments. She never thought she had to explain to the Holy Virgin the hardships she endured in the Rue Saint Jacques. Mary had experienced them.

Popular piety does not necessarily take into account the existence of the very poor, which allows them to approach Mary as a woman taking upon herself what they dream of accomplishing. We often present the figure of an innocent and pious Virgin, very far indeed from the crude realities of the world and the pangs of extreme poverty. The Virgin thus presented fulfils her destiny in distinguished solitude,

268

far removed from the very poor. Yet Mary must have been so practical and active a woman, taking full part in the rough existence of her community. I wonder what may have given rise to these images which hide the lively woman we must meet. The reactions of certain women in poverty have made me ponder this question.

These women ask me: "But what did she do that was so extraordinary? She only had one child and her husband had a job! We have six children or more to raise and feed, and social workers are always threatening to take them into foster care. My husband cannot find work. ... The Holy Virgin was pretty lucky!" Young women in Fourth World families even seem to bear that distant Mary a grudge at times. She is supposed to have all the virtues, to be endowed with all graces. She is depicted as the most beautiful and exceptional of women. What did she do to deserve this? "She's such a big deal. She never sinned? So what! It's easy to do things right when one is well-off." Where was her merit, after all, since she was safe and invulnerable? Depending on our social condition, we see the representations of Mary with different eyes. The images created by love and faith in other social strata may well estrange from her women submerged in poverty. And if the very poorest do not recognise the Blessed Virgin, is she really the Blessed Virgin at all?

The Virgin acknowledged in the Fourth World is the woman of flesh and blood, solidly rooted in the realities of her time. Solidly rooted in poverty, therefore, and not soaring in some easy, protected situation. She is not a Virgin reinterpreted according to the tastes of any given age. She steps straight out of the Gospel. Fourth World families have not shaped her to their convenience, on the contrary! Mary from the Gospel is much more demanding than any of the images made of her. She is irrefutable, firmly planted in her own world and colliding head on with all its misfortunes. She is demanding because she faces them herself to the bitter end. No doubt, her heart is open to all, she is not vindictive, but she is a fighter. She is filled with tenderness for all, but her tenderness is not of that affected quality so often ascribed to Christians. Hers is the firm tenderness of women in the habit of coming to grips with life. She is the first among the poor proclaimed blessed.

I feel the families are right in seeing Mary this way, full of liveliness, enthusiasm and a sense of action. If not, she would be a woman praising the Lord by mouth only, not by deeds, nor through her entire being. Submissive but passive, what would have been her place among the blessed, the architects of the Kingdom? Our love for the Virgin and our desire to see her as the mother of all humanity, it is true, have prompted us to proclaim her Our Lady of the Poor. Yet we should not consider this role a supplementary attribute, the poor being her children also . . . If Mary had not been first, and by her very essence, queen of the poor, she could not have become queen of all humanity. Christ could redeem all humanity by actually taking on Himself the condition of the wretched. Would the Virgin have been satisfied with a merely symbolic poverty that had no real hold on her?

Extremely poor women around me have forced me to formulate these questions clearly. They are not meant to set traps for the better-off, for the poor rarely set traps. The questions spring from practical experience. Poverty and misery represent such terribly concrete situations, it requires such matter-of-factness and obstinacy to master them. One needs so much energy and willpower if one wants *moreover* to take part in a struggle on behalf of one's neighbours. If one does not resist, one sinks. And only resisting is not enough, if one wants to create justice in one's environment. One has to surpass oneself. The question is whether we see Mary as shaped by these realities or if we consider her placed above human hardships, outside people's history as it were, and specially protected by God.

Once again, the answers are not for me to give. But I witness how Fourth World families strip the history of Mary of Nazareth of certain interpretations spun around her over the ages. These families journey through the Gospel, poor and unencumbered. And as they go along, they seem to confirm that the humble grasp what is hidden from the learned. This is as it should be, since Jesus has promised them as much. All through my priesthood, I have seen the eyes of the very poor rendering the Gospel all at once luminous, infinitely imposing and perfectly accessible. Their Mary fills us with overwhelming admiration and love. She is so real and so impressive in her radiant humanity.

We cannot fathom the power this mother of God possesses to lead the poor to God, to sustain their courage to surpass themselves on the way, to sustain especially the courage of the women. For they have an unfathomed need to be supported, as had Mary when the Angel visited her. The way in which God strengthened her faith teaches us an essential lesson: "Behold your cousin Elisabeth. She also conceived in her old age . . . because no work shall be impossible with God." These are the kind of words that can be taken into account by a woman in poverty, impregnated with a history, rather than with abstract ideas. Such a woman relies on real facts woven into a history, rather than on theoretical proof as would intellectuals. God, who knows the poor, speaks accordingly, "Go visit Elisabeth and you will know that it is I who talk to you." Mary loses no time, she hastens to the high country to greet Elisabeth and Zacharias. When she finds Elisabeth pregnant, her joy overflows. Come what may, God is her Saviour, He will keep His promise. I have always felt myself accountable for this lesson and I have never ceased to speak about Mary in poverty areas in the same way: "Go visit Mary, she will be able to tell you that God is with you. Go and see the mother next door too. She surpasses herself day after day. Mary is with her and with you."

No doubt the Virgin Mary will need to think back many times on the moments passed with the Angel. She will have to recall again and again, "God spoke to me. All that comes to me is according to His will and He will keep His word." For her faith will be sorely tried, anxiety setting in at the news of Herod's jealous pursuit. The shepherds singing God's glory, the three wise men kneeling before Jesus, the lowliest and the most wealthy united in common jubilation—they will be the last sign of God's tenderness for a long time. A convincing sign, to be sure. The shepherds leaving their flocks at night to praise the Lord are a true miracle, the work of the angels. A shepherd watches his sheep more closely at night than by day, as wild animals and bandits lie in wait. What a terrible risk they took, certain to lose their humble jobs if the owner discovered a loss! Shepherding, often the last job a person could hope for, was considered an impure occupation. They could hardly find anything lowlier, unless they became bandits themselves. Having a rough occupation, having to deal with the brutalities of brigandage, those employed in this way were accused of godlessness. They were certainly not in the habit of singing praise. That they came to the cave so joyfully could only be the work of God. It proved that they were unjustly rejected, since their hearts were pure. God delivering the humble! What infinite happiness for Mary!

Besides, the shepherds filled with wonder are going to run right and left, spreading the news among equally poor families all around. We may rest assured that Mary and the child Jesus lacked nothing while staying in the cave. The shepherds must have sung even more when they returned to their flocks, because they themselves had done all they could to protect this family from need. Mary will stock within her heart all that the coming of the shepherds really meant. She will take it with her through life and meditate on it. The Wise Men will also come, unaware as yet that they will bring disaster to the people. For the moment, the rich and the learned follow the poor on their way to the Messiah. Thus God's promise has already come true.

Has this foretaste of the Kingdom been blotted out by the news of the massacre of the innocent? Who can imagine its horror! Must God's plan be realised at the cost of such atrocities? Mary, so committed to the liberation of her people, what may she have said to the Lord in those days? She must have shared so deeply the desperation of Rachel mourning over her children, who had been despised, undesired, judged pernicious and savagely murdered. Mary's own son, born in an ocean of blood—did the Virgin imagine that she was thus to become the mother of all children in extreme poverty throughout the world, all equally pursued, suspected of being baneful, controlled, ill-treated, hypocritically abandoned to die from hunger, or simply killed before seeing the light of day? The children of extreme poverty, the children of population groups of no economic interest, the children of families who are a burden on our assistance, our charities and development aid, remain a menace to the well-off, through the ages and up to our days. Herod has not our manner of persecuting them. He practises cruelty openly, with no cunning references to development, mothers' health or world demography. Later, things will be done differently. The wealthy will rule over the poor in more subtle ways, letting them die of hunger, or encouraging abortion and sterilisation while the better-off keep for themselves expensive means to give birth to test-tube babies of their own choice. But the lamentation and weeping foretold by Jeremy continue. "And Rachel is crying for her children; she refuses to be comforted because they are dead." (Matthew 2, 18)

Mary, our Lady of the children of poverty, must have felt more strongly than before the immense responsibility that would fall on her. But what sorrow to learn her role this way, through the poor Jewish mothers of the humble town of Bethlehem, where most women lived in penury. They are her close ones, her kin. This is how Mary's own painful reconversion begins, as she discovers day by day what Simeon's frightening prophecy really meant: "This child is chosen by God for the destruction and salvation of many in Israel. He will be a sign from God which many people will speak against, and so reveal their secret thoughts. And sorrow, like a sharp sword, will break your own heart." (Luke 2, 34-35) Jesus would live and die so that all mothers of children in poverty, humiliated and tortured for their children's sake, might be restored to honour. But Mary could not foresee the dreadful sorrow she would have to bear that the Saviour might live. She would have to repeat over and over, "Behold the handmaid of the Lord."

We do not know how Mary learnt the terrible tidings, nor how she lived in Egypt. Children of the Fourth World are puzzled by our ignorance. Did we not try to find out? Here is the Son of God, and yet we let matters rest? "How did they live, how did migrant workers live in Egypt? Did they have lodgings, find a job? Wasn't the baby put into foster care?" Such were the questions volleyed at me in catechism class and I felt at a loss. I was obliged to tell them I knew next to nothing and I began wondering if knowing about life in ancient Egypt was the sole business of scholars. What efforts did Catholic universities make to tell the life of the infant Jesus to children in poverty?

The least I could do was to meditate with these children eager to learn about this mysterious Mary in Egypt. I could tell them of her courage, enduring exile to save her son. This way they could recognise something they experienced in their own families, but for which they had no name: the endurance, the pluck of their own mothers. Of course, no woman can resemble the Mother of God, but what similarities in their lives and reactions! So many children are hidden even today behind a partition or in an attic. How many families hastily leave a slum at night to prevent the authorities from laying hands on the children! And, the danger averted one more time, life must go on. Mothers of Fourth World families, the Virgin Mary in Egypt, all must somehow succeed in going through the simple motions of everyday life. When one has no means whatsoever, one must invent them from day to day. "How shall I clothe the child? What shall I feed my family tonight? Where can I scrounge some vegetables for soup? How can I help my husband wash up, how can I keep his suit clean? He will have no pride left with these worn-out shoes he is wearing. . . ." These are the constant worries of mothers who must see that life remains livable from dawn to dusk, while the night serves for inventing what can be done tomorrow. Keeping life bearable sometimes means simply having the will to live for one's family, to continue being a mother who knows how to comfort and encourage, when life has nothing else to offer. In fact this is what being a mother in extreme poverty means: remaining the one who knows how to find the words and invent the small gestures that will sustain husband and children despite the worst deprivations. This is the last role remaining when all else has collapsed.

There is no choice really. "Either I hold on, or I might as well kill myself," a young mother said to me. She had come from Brittany with her husband and four children. Her husband had the new-born baby in his arms, while she carried their only piece of luggage, a cardboard box holding some baby clothes. They settled down in one of the Nissen huts of the Camp for the Homeless. Madame Meulan set out to create a home and home life, mainly with cardboard, rags, and old newspapers. Every meal was made up of noodles. The social worker lamented, but the children were always smiling. One day, however, Mme. Meulan broke down. She took to drink and the humble home went to rack and ruin. Only then did it become evident what a miracle she had achieved up to that time. When she gave up, all fell apart, the children ran wild, her husband went out with other women. For years, by her sole willpower, the mother had achieved the impossible to maintain her family.

In the Fourth World, all mothers achieve the impossible, as Mary must have done in exile. No woman can have Mary's strength, and some break down and remain broken for long periods of time. This is what happened to Madame Meulan, who soon saw her children taken to the Paris public assistance "depot." Most mothers resist, and those who give up one day take hold of themselves again, making continuous efforts to climb uphill once more. But these efforts, for lack of means, are so humble that we can hardly see them. Who notices the worn mattress that has replaced the old rags that used to serve as a bed for the children? But such humble gestures are noticed by the family, the children suddenly returning to school and the husband starting to look for a job again. It is not the mattress as such that counts, it is the mother taking up her struggle again that makes the difference. The neighbourhood also takes notice. They can tell when a woman gives up and when she overcomes her despair. In fact the whole dynamic of social life in the poverty areas around our western cities stems from the women. And when the mother next door is up early, lighting her stove, everyone around has a little more courage.

Mothers of courage, carrying on their slender shoulders a people of courage, how eminently destined to meet Mary they seem to me. They have experienced so much insecurity, so many abandonments. They can sense the Virgin's anguish. They have resisted so much injustice and dishonour. They can recognise offhand the gestures, the signs of this resistance in the lives of other women. I am always profoundly touched when witnessing meetings between very poor families of different countries. Men and women separated by language barriers look at one another and communicate. Especially the women seem proud and happy. They sit down together spontaneously and speak without reticence about their aspirations and problems. "We made friends with the London families right away," says a mother from Belgium. "You made friends? So you could talk?" "Oh, as for talking, we only knew what they wanted to say after the interpreters told us. But we could tell straight away that they were fine women!"

Among the very poor, the women especially have a mysterious language among themselves. It is made up of signs: demeanour, a way of dressing, when all one has are the worn clothes—either too large or too small—handed out by a clothing centre. There is a way to wear cast-off clothes with dignity. And there is a way of looking at another without astonishment, the gesture of offering a seat: come and sit with me—glances and gestures rarely encountered elsewhere. Even at church, at a first communion or a christening, the faithful look at you with astonishment and somehow keep you at bay. When extremely poor families meet, their faces and bodies betray their misery, but their demeanour and gestures express their refusal of injustice. This dogged resistance is not necessarily effective, its results are not always convincing and a stranger to poverty cannot discern these women's passionate quest for justice. He does not see that even without always knowing it, they follow Mary. Outsiders often notice that they are "very nervous." Doctors prescribe tranquillisers for them. In all areas of extreme poverty in France and throughout western Europe, the will of women to refuse and to contend is lulled to sleep. Still, they recognise one another and are outstandingly capable of recognising Mary. They can tell the matchless intensity of her passion, of her sharing of her people's agonising destiny. More than all, she was true to the God of the Bible and paid the price of

279

her fidelity. Therefore, "God loved her more than the others, that's only normal," says a young Dutch woman.

To the eyes of these severely deprived women, the majesty of the Virgin is rooted in life's reality. God's choice was no arbitrary one, it was based on facts, on a "true story," as the women say. Mary embodied the hope of the Jewish people and of its justness. A just woman herself, she sided with the poor, of course, but she sided primarily with the righteous. She embodied all at once poverty, faith, wisdom and the entire history of the forefathers. In her life, the poor were at the heart of her faith, and she also placed them at the heart of her people's history. Their liberation would be the sign that all her people had found the way back to the Almighty's goodness. To the Fourth World families, Mary is not just a mediatrix between humanity and God. She also creates justice and therefore reconciliation among people. This was God's plan, of course. But Fourth World women are happy to discover this plan through the Virgin who places them at the very heart of humanity. Mary does not divide them nor make them rise up *against* other women. She brings them what they crave—dignity in peace. "She honours us," the women say, "and we never conclude Holy Mass without praying, 'Our Lady of those who have naught, Our Lady of those who are naught, Our Lady of those who come to naught, Our Lady of all people, Our Lady of all glory, pray for us.'" "If she forgave," said one woman, "then all of us can forgive."

Mary's existence, a constant mediation, this is how we see her life evolve all through the Gospel. She continues to journey to Jerusalem for Passover. With Joseph, she remains fully part of the life of her people, where the poor, the wretched and the rich, the righteous and the unjust, those who hold learning and power all mingle. The paths of Zachea on the sycamore, of Nicodemus, of the hostile priests and the blind beggars all intertwine. Leaving some would mean leaving all. The Holy Family cannot go underground. It is bound to stay in the midst of this motley crossroads of humanity. Mary will find it all the harder to live out her passion for the humble and to share it more and more intensely with Jesus and Joseph. Be it in Nazareth or on the road to Jerusalem, she is always nurturing the Magnificat in her heart. But where is the victory? Wherever she turns her eyes, she sees famished men, sitting at the roadside, desperate at seeing the eleventh hour pass without their being called to the vineyard. Each year, their numbers grow and they look a little more exhausted.

To the Temple, the Virgin brings her unadulterated respect for the priesthood. In her eyes, the priesthood is first and foremost a divine institution. Unlike us, she was able to differentiate between the priesthood God had established and the possible shortcomings of those called upon to assume it. To turn away from it or denigrate it would mean affecting Christ and annulling His coming into the world. Yet Mary sees many priests who do not shoulder their mission to free the poor. She is no doubt always with those women who offer the smallest sacrifice— "two turtle doves." She witnesses the little account taken of them. In fact, Mary can no more accept the false god of Jerusalem than she can break away from the Temple to join the Zealots. How did she manage to teach Jesus that the essential thing was not the splendour of the divine services nor the number of sacrificial lambs offered, but the prayer abiding in people's hearts? For I feel sure that Jesus received this teaching from Mary who herself could not pray to her Lord, the Saviour of the humble, other than in the deepest secret of her heart.

Did Mary sometimes falter? For me, this is unthinkable. For the sake of God and of her son, she could afford no hesitation. She could not afford it because of the child she had to educate and because of her husband. But then what faith must have strengthened her! That is something Fourth World families can also imagine. They are unable themselves to keep desperation and bitterness at bay. The Virgin sets the example, and in areas of extreme poverty she therefore appears even more admirable than elsewhere. Her alliance with God, manifest in her unfaltering faith and hope, appears a truly unfathomable mystery here. How does she manage never to weaken as she gradually discovers all the cruel realities which lie in store for Christ, and which she will therefore have to endure herself? God has placed along her way all the indications that must guide her: the contempt encountered in Bethlehem, the flight to Egypt, Rachel's mourning. . . . Step by step, she must learn, herself, Isaiah's prophesy about the man of sorrows for which she will have to prepare her son. It is a prophecy forever engraved in the very heart of the Church, because Mary accepted to become this man's mother, condemned to endure what was foretold for Him.

The people reply,
"Who would have believed what we now report?
Who could have seen the Lord's hand in this?
It was the will of the Lord that His servant
should grow like a plant taking root in dry ground.
He had no dignity or beauty
to make us take notice of Him.
There was nothing attractive about Him,
nothing that would draw us to Him.
We despised Him and rejected Him;
He endured suffering and pain.
No one would even look at Him—
we ignored Him as if He were nothing.
"But He endured the suffering
that should have been ours,
the pain that we should have borne.
All the while we thought that His suffering
was punishment sent by God.
But because of our sins He was wounded,
beaten because of the evil we did.
We are healed by the punishment He suffered,
made whole by the blows He received.
All of us were like sheep that were lost,
each of us going his own way.
But the Lord made the punishment fall on Him,
the punishment all of us deserved.
"He was treated harshly, but endured it humbly;
He never said a word.
Like a lamb about to be slaughtered,
like a sheep about to be sheared,

He never said a word.
He was arrested and sentenced and led off to die,
and no one cared about His fate.
He was put to death for the sins of our people.
He was placed in a grave with evil men,
He was buried with the rich,
even though He had never committed a crime
or ever told a lie."
The Lord says, "It was my will that He should
      suffer;

His death was a sacrifice to bring forgiveness.
And so He will see His descendants;
He will live a long life,
and through Him, my purpose will succeed.
After a life of suffering, He will again have joy;
He will know that He did not suffer in vain.
My devoted servant, with whom I am pleased,
will bear the punishment of many
and for His sake I will forgive them.
And so I will give Him a place of honour,
a place among great and powerful men.
He willingly gave His life
and shared the fate of evil men."

(Isaiah 53)

"He was oppressed and afflicted, yet He did not
open His mouth. . . . And it pleased the Lord to
bruise Him." It is one thing to hear the words, and
another to be the mother who will have to see her son
endure such sorrows. Mary has spent all her life
strengthening herself and Jesus, feeling the menace
but knowing neither when nor how it was to become

a terrible and unthinkable reality. No doubt at times she conceived a mad hope, when life appeared to grow easier, Jesus "going forth in wisdom before God and all people." Since God and the people were good, perhaps all would not go as she feared! How wonderful a reprieve, seeing Jesus among the crowd, healing the most wretched and declaring them saved. There goes Christ, living to the full the love of the humble she has instilled in Him. Yet God, from then on, does not cease to send warnings: prepare yourself, the fatal outcome cannot be averted. God Himself prepares Mary, allowing her to take part in the developments. The joy of the poor is always followed by the vengeance of the mighty. From refusal to denunciation, from denunciation to condemnation, they plot His downfall. And what to say of Mary's confounding discovery that the just will not defend Him? He is not the one they were awaiting to set their people free. His manner is far too disconcerting, even to them. While Mary's fear turns to anguish and finally to terrifying certainty, she has to submit to the will of God over and over. Even Joseph can no longer help her, and the day comes when the only person she still counts on asks, "Who is my mother?" Even Jesus is hers no longer. She is alone and, like Rachel, she cannot be comforted.

Christ's triumphant entry into Jerusalem can delude her no more. In her eyes, it can have been but a brief moment of grace. "Blessed is He who comes in the name of the Lord." To her it is an ultimate reassurance from God, "Fear not, He is the King, I shall keep my word." But Mary now knows that not a single line of

Isaiah's prophecy will be spared her son or herself. She too must live through Calvary till the bitter end, her feet carrying her to Golgotha. "I am still your handmaid, oh, Lord, why have you forsaken me?" What other words could she utter on her way to Golgotha but her son's words on the Cross? At the foot of the Cross, the mother of Christ herself sank into death. With her son, step by step, she had come to understand that complete suffering represented complete refusal of injustice. Christ had chosen total suffering as the only weapon against sin, oppression and misery. Even without yet realising the ultimate consequences, she had taught Him herself that the pain of being ignored, despised and rejected had not undermined the strength of the people of Israel. On the contrary, it had braced their resistance against the oppressor. Nor had Mary ever ceased to be the woman from the House of David, strong and drawing strength from adversity. This is how she could carry to the foot of the Cross all the burden of misfortunes of her people and of the whole world: the burdens of hunger, sickness, misery, and hatred. She was not only the symbol, but the very reality of suffering humanity. In the name of all humanity, she could offer to God her own total suffering, the cup drained to the dregs. She had nothing left to offer but her own life led to the utmost limits of sorrow.

Christ could therefore say to her, "Woman, here is your son," and to John, "Here is your mother." On the Cross, thanks to Mary, Christ could thus found the Church. John and Mary at His feet, without any doubt, were the Church. Christ Himself, nailed to the Cross between the two thieves who witnessed

286

His condition—all at once slave and Son of God—was the Church. Over His head the inscription, "King of the Jews"; at His feet, Mary offering her life of sorrow, and John, the disciple who loved Him—was this not the Church rising up on Golgotha, humiliated and battered? This is how the Church will stand at the centre of the world for all time.

Mary was first to participate totally in the salvation of humanity, in the death of the Saviour, the Eucharist, the perfect and total refusal of the absence of love, of oppression and misery. Christ, offering His body for nourishment, imposes no condition but that we believe that each time, over and over throughout the ages, He commits Himself, so that people may share, so that they may share the same meal, the same banquet, the same joy and one and the same love which will overthrow the order of the world. The poor will be satiated. Mary believed it to the point of giving her own life too. Having accomplished her task, she remains forever the Mother of God, Queen of Heaven, but also the Mother of the Church on earth, Mother of the Church forever persecuted for glorifying Christ miserable, risen from the dead, Mother of the poorest, as she was in the beginning, and ever shall be, world without end.

Acknowledgements

I should specially like to thank the following for
their contribution to this meditation:

Alwine de Vos van Steenwijk, Gabrielle Erpicum,
Germaine Quéméré, André Modave,
Pierre Davienne,
Jean-Claude Caillaux
and all the volunteers of the International
Movement ATD Fourth World
with whom, for twenty-five years now,
I have been living the Gospel of Jesus Christ at the
heart of extreme poverty.

BY THE SAME AUTHOR

Pologne, que deviennent les sous-proletaires (with
   Alwine de Vos van Steenwijk), Les Editions
   Science et Service, 1981.
Les Pauvres Sont l'Eglise, Le Centurion, 1983.
Paroles Pour Demain, Desclée. de Brouwer, 1985.
Les Pauvres, Rencontre du Vrai Dieu, Les Editions du
   Cerf, 1986.

Also available in French:
   Pere Joseph, by Alwine de Vos van Steenwijk, Les
   Editions Science & Service, 1989.

BY THE SAME AUTHOR